THE CROSS IN ENGLISH LIFE AND DEVOTION

The Cross in English Life and Devotion

BY

GORDON HUELIN

FOREWORD BY
THE ARCHBISHOP OF CANTERBURY

THE FAITH PRESS
7 Tufton Street, London, SW1P 3QD
MOREHOUSE-BARLOW CO. INC., NEW YORK, U.S.A.

FIRST PUBLISHED IN 1972

© *Gordon Huelin, 1972*

PRINTED IN GREAT BRITAIN
in 10pt. Times type
BY THE FAITH PRESS LTD.
LEIGHTON BUZZARD

SBN 7164 0215 7

TO
JOHN

CONTENTS

FOREWORD

I DO not know of another book which deals with the theme about which Dr. Gordon Huelin has with my encouragement chosen to write. Through the centuries in this country the Crucifixion of our Lord has been represented in painting, in sculpture, in poetry, in drama, in popular customs as well as in preaching, worship and prayer. This book gives us a series of historical glimpses of the place of the Cross in these different aspects of our English tradition, and it does so in such a way as to illustrate the meaning of the Cross for the lives of men and women. In a remarkable way the book combines the study of history, art and literature with a practical Christian message.

The scholarly reader will find in these pages, with the aid of the notes at the end of each chapter, material for a fascinating pursuit of historical knowledge. But so little is the scholarship obtruded that the book will have a host of readers who value it for its challenging presentation of the message of the Cross to the heart, the conscience and the imagination. They will share my own gratitude for an unusual and rewarding piece of work.

✝ MICHAEL CANTUAR:

PREFACE

AMONG those to whom I must express my thanks for help in the making of this book are the Trustees of the British Museum who have generously allowed me to use a magnificent line-drawing from the Ramsey Psalter, Harl. Ms. 2904, as the cover illustration.

Thanks are also due to the Oxford University Press for permission to quote the lines on p. 22 from Charles Williams's *Judgement at Chelmsford*, and those on p. 61 from David Gascoyne's *Ecce Homo*, also to the Community of the Resurrection for the last verse of hymn No. 71 in *100 Hymns for Today* on p. 49. Should I have been guilty of infringing any copyright, I ask pardon.

Of the books which I have consulted two deserve special mention: W. O. Stevens, *The Cross in the Life and Literature of the Anglo-Saxons*, which first sparked off my interest in the subject, and Rosemary Woolf, *The English Religious Lyric in the Middle Ages* which proved to be a mine of information on many matters.

While the notes serve as an indication of my debt to others, and as a guide for any who may wish to do further study, they are deliberately placed at the end of each chapter so that the majority of readers may skip them.

G.H.

Holy Cross Day, 1971

I

THE FACT OF THE CROSS

(i)

'THAT year is looked upon as unhappy and hateful to all good men.' Those words were written, not of the year of our Lord's crucifixion but of one almost exactly six centuries later; and they concerned a small island at the farthest extremity of the then known world.

The Christian Faith which was brought to Britain long before by unknown missionaries and traders, had once more flourished, and through the example of kings and the endeavours of priests many had been won for Christ. Suddenly, however, in the kingdom of Northumbria there came a terrible setback. A Welsh invader, Cadwallon, though professing Christianity, proved himself to be a merciless tyrant ravaging the land and sparing neither woman nor children whom he tortured and put to death. Bishop Paulinus, who previously had been so devoted in his efforts to set forth the way of salvation through the cross, now either through fear or despair forsook his people and fled, leaving only a deacon behind him. He took with him the large golden cross that had borne witness to the faith: a faith which was again threatened with extinction. It was one of those grim moments in our island's history: a year 'unhappy and hateful to all good men'.

Then the miracle happened, and the downcast and persecuted Christians of Northumbria found a saviour in the man later to be known as *Saint* Oswald. As he was about to do battle with his adversaries at a place a few miles north of Hexham, Oswald first set up a wooden cross, and then kneeling before it with his all too meagre army, he made what is the earliest prayer offered in front of an English cross that has come down to us:

'May Almighty God in his mercy defend us from an arrogant and savage enemy: for he knows that we have undertaken a just war for the safety of our nation'.

The Venerable Bede, to whom we are so deeply indebted for our knowledge of the early English Church, has left us a vivid picture of the scene.[1] He tells of the rough wooden cross put together in the utmost haste; of the hole in which it was to stand being feverishly dug; and of the devout Oswald in all the ardour of his newly-found faith grasping the Christian standard with both hands and holding it upright while his soldiers heaped the earth around it until at last it was firmly fixed in the ground. With the light of dawn, the forces of Cadwallon came down like waves; but they broke in vain against the rock of that cross 'towering o'er the wrecks of time'. Oswald's prayer was answered, and the tyrant and his army were utterly routed by the defenders of the faith. The rough wooden cross so hastily set up had decided the fate of Britain. Little wonder that the place of victory should for long afterwards be called the heavenly field.

Few of the many thrilling episodes in the early history of Christianity in this island can match that one; and even though Oswald's wooden cross has long since gone the story of it makes a splendid starting-point to our theme—the cross in English life and devotion.

(ii)

'They crucified him': that was a fact which the earliest disciples of Jesus could never forget. As they looked back to the events of the first Good Friday there must always have remained for them a sense of shame: shame above all at the miserable part which they themselves had played in the grim drama. It was not enough to lay the blame on the Roman authorities or the religious leaders of their own nation and to say '*they* crucified him'. For always, deep down within

14

themselves, the voice of conscience would make itself heard: 'It was not simply *they* who crucified him; we had our part in it as well; *we* crucified him'.

Christian men and women know very well the feelings of such remorse: the kind of feelings to which Augustine of Hippo gave expression when he uttered the bitter cry 'Too late have I come to love thee'. In spite of the remark of W. H. Auden in a recently published book concerning the scene of Golgotha: 'None of us, I'm certain, will imagine himself as one of the disciples, cowering in an agony of spiritual despair and physical terror',[2] most of those who struggle along the way of Christian discipleship do in fact recognise themselves as in precisely that position.

If Christ had not been the person he was, then the behaviour of his friends on Maundy Thursday and Good Friday, when one of them betrayed him, another denied him, and all forsook him and fled, could very easily have led to the break up of the community. But just because he was the person that he was, their own state was in many respects worse, and the cross stood as a perpetual reminder of their sorry condition. Nor could they forget that crucifixion, death on a cross, was the most shameful form of death which any man could suffer: the punishment reserved for slaves, brigands and the lowest type of criminals. Did not their own Law say that everyone who hung on a tree was cursed? Paul might talk in his letter to the Galatians about 'glorying in the cross of our Lord Jesus Christ', just as we may sing such lines as:

'Forbid it Lord that I should boast
Save in the Cross of Christ my God',

and say such words as: 'Grant us so to glory in the cross of Christ, that we may gladly suffer shame and loss';[3] but for the first three hundred years of the Church's history the followers of Christ found it anything but easy to glory in the cross.

Then two things happened: first, there was that vision

experienced by the emperor Constantine the Great in the year 312 when as he was about to engage in battle against the pagans he saw the cross over the sun in the sky and inscribed on it in shining letters the words: 'In this sign conquer'; secondly, a few years afterwards, there was the discovery made by his mother, Helena, during a pilgrimage to the holy places of Palestine, of the cross on which Christ had actually suffered crucifixion.

Those two remarkable events changed everything. Instead of being an emblem of shame and disgrace the cross became transformed into one of glory and honour. From then onwards, its praises were proclaimed in hymns and prayers, and each year on Good Friday it became the object of veneration in a most solemn ceremony in every church in Christendom. So men were brought to see in the cross the very reverse of shame and disgrace. More and more the cross entered into their everyday lives, with the result that they wanted to have it always before them and could not be reminded of it too often. A man stretching out his arms in prayer; a bird spreading its wings as it flew in the air; a ship at sea riding the waves: all of these and more besides became symbols of the cross of Christ as far as Christians were concerned.

(iii)

'The medieval Christian', it has been said, 'was a man of one event. The passion of Christ was his daily meditation. Over the whole medieval world lay the broad shadow of the cross.' [4]

Inside the church itself every single ceremony and sacrament was accompanied by the making of the sacred sign as it is for many Christians still today: from the cross impressed on the forehead of the child in Baptism and that made by the priest over the bread and wine in the Eucharist, to the cross made in pronouncing absolution to the penitent and that bestowed on the bride and bridegroom in Marriage. In the very centre of the church building high above all, there hung the great rood with the figure of Christ hanging on the cross, and beneath him on either side his Mother and John; while on its walls around there were probably painted scenes of the passion, and in its stained glass windows or wooden carvings there might well be passion emblems.

Even in books used in the church's worship the cross was given a special place: for it is from the magnificent tenth century Psalter which once belonged to the abbey of Ramsey in Huntingdonshire that there comes that simple line drawing of the figure of Christ on the cross, his Mother with bowed head on the one side, and John with a scroll containing his own testimony 'This is the disciple who bears witness' on the other. It has been said of this illustration that 'truly nothing finer of its kind had yet been produced on the Continent or in England'.[5]

Simple worshippers might not be able to follow a great deal of the service, but at the most solemn moment when Christ's death was represented once again in the consecration at the Eucharist they were encouraged to use this fine prayer from the *Lay Folks Mass Book:*

> 'Praised be thou, King,
> And blessed be thou, King;
> For all thy gifts good,
> And thanked be thou, King;
> Jesu, all my joying,
> That for me spilt thy blood,
> And died upon the rood,
> Thou give me grace to sing
> The song of thy praising'.[6]

Outside the church the cross was given a scarcely less prominent place; in fact in very early days it often had to serve instead of a religious building. It is worth remembering that what later on became a great English cathedral or abbey may have started from the humblest of beginnings, a few folk gathered together round a simple open-air cross. When

17

Willibald, whom we remember now as one of our renowned missionaries to the continent of Europe in the eighth century, was three years old he was solemnly dedicated by his parents to the service of God at the foot of a cross which stood near their home in what is now Hampshire. The reason, as his biographer explains, was that it was customary among the Saxon people on the estates of nobles or gentry to have for the use of those who made a point of attending daily prayers, not a church but the sign of the holy cross set up aloft and consecrated to the Lord.[7] Place-names such as Crosby and Crossthwaites in Northumberland suggest that these were originally settlements where more than one such cross was erected.

Again, men were accustomed to having their everyday tools of trade blessed with the sign of the cross, as well as the fields where they sowed and reaped, and the boats from which they fished. On every side the cross greeted their eyes: in monuments such as the two magnificent Anglo-Saxon crosses to be seen at Bewcastle in Northumberland and at Ruthwell just over the Scottish border in Dumfriesshire;[8] as market-crosses in the centre of towns and villages; in the preaching cross around which men and women would gather to hear the message of their redemption; as boundary marks, or at the crossing of a ford, or simply standing by the highway.

Sometimes a cross would be set up for a special object, like that which in the early sixteenth century was placed in the churchyard in front of St. Margaret Pattens in the city of London, so that the citizens might bring to it their gifts of money for the rebuilding of the church. Even though that cross has long since disappeared it is still remembered by the street name of Rood Lane.

Were there men who were critical of all this? An anonymous English writer of the fourteenth century, in considering the cross in relation to the Second Commandment answers that it is a laudable custom to have the image of Christ on the cross: 'that we in having mind on the death of Christ may overcome the temptations and the venom of the fiend, the old serpent'.[9] A passage in *Dives and Pauper,* a moral treatise by an unnamed author published in London towards the end of the fifteenth century, tells us that: 'for this reason are crosses by the way, that when folk passing see the cross, they should think on him that died on the cross, and worship him above all things'.[10]

How right was the person who described the religion of England in the days prior to the Reformation as the religion of the cross. One wonders whether greater devotion for it was to be found anywhere else in the medieval world.

(iv)

Frequently in the medieval literary and artistic portrayals of the crucifixion of Christ there were elements which seem strange to us, and undoubtedly there were many grotesque exaggerations. When however people feel as strongly about a subject as they felt about this one there is a natural tendency to exaggerate.

A Passion play performed in the Middle Ages in some English market-place might contain what appears to some people today as rough horse-play and buffoonery utterly out of keeping with the solemn theme. There is a strange prudishness still in these matters, although this does not manifest itself about other things in life. It should be remembered that the lighter touches were deliberately introduced in order to relieve the tension and the emotions of the audience who felt so deeply about the sufferings of Christ.

Hardly surprisingly, there were also many foolish and superstitious stories concerning the cross; like that of the nun who was supposed to have been carried off by the devil because she had eaten a lettuce without first of all making the holy sign.[11] But these were no more foolish than are many of the secular superstitions to which some of us still cling in the twentieth century.

Nevertheless, it was because of these and other crudities that there came the time when men thought it right and proper to rid themselves of the cross both inside and outside their churches. The great rood which for so long had hung high over all was torn down, broken up and burned. The many beautiful wall paintings of Christ in his passion were white-washed over. The monuments in churchyards, in fields and on highways were desecrated. The market-cross, the preaching cross and even the cross on the church steeple were all destroyed.

To be privileged to handle the original accounts kept by the churchwardens of numberless parishes up and down England during those years, in which the payments made to work-men for 'taking down', 'washing out' or 'defacing' the rood are so regularly set down in the actual ink of the time, is to live momentarily once more through those troubled years. And to gaze on the wonderful figure of Christ, mutilated though it is but still bearing the Latin inscription 'He made himself obedient to death, even the death of the cross', which was then hidden and remained so until four hundred years later it was unexpectedly dug up beneath the hall of the Mercers' Company in the very heart of the city of London, and is now given an honoured place at the entrance to the Company's chapel, is to be made aware for oneself of the faith both of its maker and of those for whom it was once an object of prayerful devotion.

On certain principles the English Church refused to aban-don its ancient witness. When, for example, the Puritans called for the omission of the sign of the cross from the Prayer Book service of infant baptism, the Anglicans made it plain that the Church of England had deliberately retained this sign: 'accounting it a lawful outward ceremony and honourable badge whereby the infant is dedicated to the service of him that died upon the cross'.[12]

(v)

Prejudice and wanton destruction as far as the cross is concerned here in England are now for the most part a past memory. Once again the cross has been brought back into our churches. Year by year on Good Friday it is made the centre of Christian devotion by various means. In some of our large towns and cities a huge wooden cross is carried through the streets as an act of united witness in a non-violent demonstration. At the village of Swimbridge in north Devon, it has been the custom for the past eight years for young people to meet in church for prayers at an early hour on Good Friday morning, and from there to carry a full-size wooden cross to the top of a nearby hill, where it stands throughout the day to be seen for miles around.[13] Even many of our brothers in the Free Church tradition have now overcome their former fears, and find it of spiritual benefit to have before them in their places of worship a simple wooden cross.

We can rejoice that the days of desecration are over; nevertheless, in spite of this and of those Good Friday acts of witness, we can hardly fail to ask whether the cross has the place which it held for so long in the life of the ordinary Englishman. So far from being on every side in our land today it is conspicuous by its absence, as no Christian who has travelled through certain parts of Europe can fail to be painfully aware when he returns home. Even in places where not so many years ago the cross was to be seen it has now gone. In central London before the Second World War there stood two churches on the outside walls of which hung a crucifix bearing witness in places where that witness was desperately needed, and where some of the passers-by may have been stopped short in their evil courses by the sight of the figure of Christ their Saviour hanging there.[14] Now that witness has been removed in the interests of so-called material progress and development. There is also little need to point out how, year by year, the observance of what for the Christian believer is the most solemn day of all, Good Friday, becomes increasingly less for the majority of our countrymen, and in some industrial cities is virtually ignored.

The cross and its place in English life and devotion: is that something on which we Christians of today have to look back rather wistfully as being merely a part of our past heritage? Is it something which must be regarded now as chiefly of historic or antiquarian interest? Has the cross a message for ourselves and our contemporaries in the second half of the twentieth century, and can it be seen as being relevant to our own situation and needs?

Shall we let Thomas Ken in *Judgement at Chelmsford,* a play by Charles Williams, answer that last question on our behalf? In the play as Helena the discoverer of the true cross comes to Jerusalem, Charles Williams makes Ken say:

'It is one thing to come where the Cross is and another thing to find the Cross. Trials and vexations are God's way of bringing us to God's holy place, that is to say, to the Jerusalem that is within our souls. . . .

'But, O good people, how blessed are you if, having come to that Jerusalem, you do indeed find, by God's grace, the secret and hidden thing. For find you the Cross without you, as did that blessed lady, you shall find a precious, an inestimable treasure, the wood on which our Saviour rested without resting, the bloody, bloody wood bedewed. But find you the Cross within you as that blessed Empress also did, and you shall find Christ himself." [15]

NOTES

[1] Bede, *History of the English Church and People* (Penguin, 1955), Bk. III, 2.

[2] W. H. Auden, *A Certain World* (Faber, 1971), p. 169.

[3] Collect for Holy Cross Day, 1928 Prayer Book.

[4] B. L. Manning, *The People's Faith in the time of Wycliffe* (C.U.P. 1919), p. 25.

[5] M. Rickert, *Painting in Britain in the Middle Ages* (Penguin, 1954), p. 41. It is, of course, the illustration on the cover of this book.

[6] T. F. Simmons (ed.), *Lay Folks Mass Book* (E.E.T.S. No. 71), p. 40.

[7] C. H. Talbot, *The Anglo-Saxon Missionaries in Germany* (Sheed & Ward, 1954), p. 155

[8] G. Baldwin Brown, *The Arts in Early England: vol. 5, The Ruthwell and Bewcastle Crosses* (Murray, 1921).

[9] G. R. Owst, *Literature and Pulpit in Medieval England* (C.U.P. 1933), p. 141.

[10] A. Vallance, *Old Crosses and Lychgates* (Batsford, 1920), p. 1.

[11] R. Morris (ed.), *Legends of the Holy Rood* (E.E.T.S. No. 46), p. 169.

[12] Canons of 1604, No. 30.

[13] These details were kindly sent to me in a letter by the Rev. R. T. Gilpin, Vicar of Swimbridge.

[14] St. John's, Wilton Road and St. Mary's, Charing Cross Road.

[15] Charles Williams, *Collected Plays* (O.U.P., 1963), pp. 142–3

II

JUDGEMENT AND HOPE

(i)

THE successful restoration in recent times of many of the medieval wall paintings in our churches, which had for so long been hidden under a coat of whitewash, has taught us much about the faith and worship of our forefathers. One thing which has become apparent is the fact that the medieval Englishman was continually reminded of the Last Judgement whenever he attended his church. Some modern historians have taken it upon themselves to criticise the Church for its emphasis in this direction, and have sympathised with the poor parishioner for ever faced with the picture of demons carrying off human souls to endless torments. Whether medieval man would have felt the need of such sympathy may be questioned; for if he was presented with a picture of the judgement of sinners he also saw before him the hope of those who had striven after what was good and right.

In the church of Wymington in Bedfordshire there can be seen over the chancel arch and extending to the north and south walls of the nave one such painting of the Last Judgement.[1] The demons and all their paraphernalia are there of course; for without them no artist of the fifteenth century would have regarded the picture as complete. But within the picture itself there is the heavenly city, represented as a small town, at the gate of which stands St. Peter welcoming a party of the redeemed. What is most significant of all is that above the gate there is a shield bearing on it the five wounds of Christ. The symbolism is both moving and plain for everyone to understand: it is through the cross and Christ's sufferings upon it alone that mankind is able to enter through the gate of heaven; and in this fact lies our hope.

24

So often however, as in the painting at Wymington, this hope is to be found within the setting of judgement. In the fine Advent hymn of Charles Wesley, 'Lo! he comes with clouds descending', for example, the 'dear tokens' of Christ's passion are the 'cause of endless exultation to his ransomed worshippers', but we are not spared the reminder that 'those who set at naught and sold him, pierced and nailed him to the tree', are 'deeply wailing'.

In case this may be attributed by some as a sadistic tendency on the part of ecclesiastical artists and hymn-writers let us turn to something more down-to-earth, the *Life of Samuel Johnson*. Boswell records there how, on one occasion, the celebrated doctor was discussing with a friend, Dr. Adams, the subject of the Last Judgement, during the course of which Johnson became very vehement in expressing his opinions. At one point, Boswell intervened with the question: 'But may not a man attain to such a degree of hope as not to be uneasy from the fear of death?' To which Johnson replied: 'A man may have such a degree of hope as to keep him quiet. You see I am not quiet from the vehemence with which I talk; but I do not despair.' When Mrs. Adams felt moved to remark: 'You seem, sir, to forget the merits of our Redeemer', Johnson answered: 'Madam, I do not forget the merits of my Redeemer; but my Redeemer has said that he will set some on his right hand and some on his left'.[2]

(ii)

The imagery which surrounds the contrast between judgement and hope in relation to the cross and passion of Christ is both varied and remarkable in its character. For the first example it is necessary to turn to the Old Testament.

Those who are accustomed during Holy Week to follow the Church's liturgy day by day may be puzzled by what appears to be a strange choice on the part of the compilers of the Anglican Book of Common Prayer of a passage from the sixty-third chapter of Isaiah to serve as the Epistle for

Monday before Easter. There we see the approach of a divine figure dressed in blood-red garments who has trampled in his wrath upon his enemies, just as one would tread a wine-press.

To the question as to why this choice, the answer would seem to be that some of the Fathers of the Church, such as Cyprian, saw in this passage from Isaiah a direct reference to the passion and death of Christ. Biblical scholars nowadays may point out that the Fathers were mistaken in applying a prophecy to Christ which concerned the vengeance of God on the enemies of his own people; but the fact remains that they did so, as did also a number of later medieval writers. For these men there was no doubt that Christ was the grape-harvester who had undertaken his task single-handed; and who had come from that task stained with the juice which was symbolic of his blood.

It was a fourteenth century Franciscan, William Herebert, who wrote an English paraphrase on this passage from Isaiah:

> 'What is he this lordling that comes from the fight
> With blood-red clothing so terribly dyed?';

to which, presently, there comes the answer given by Christ himself:

> 'The wine-press I have trodden all myself alone,
> And of all mankind there was no other hope'.[3]

There we have it set down in no uncertain terms. On the one hand there is that divine wrath and judgement in the face of sin, a fact of which the Bible leaves us in no doubt. On the other hand there is hope in Christ our only redeemer.

In some continental countries, there gradually developed a grotesque idea known as the 'Mystic wine-press' in which Christ was pressed like a grape. Through such media as sculpture, stained-glass and engravings, he was pictured as being so crushed by the wine-press that the blood poured forth from his feet and hands and side. That blood was received in a chalice, usually held by two angels; and for the faithful this naturally came to represent the sacrament of the Eucharist.

While excesses of this kind do not seem to have made much appeal to the people of our own country, yet the symbol of Christ and the wine-press featured in at least one prayer which they used. It was addressed to Jesus, 'the true and fruitful vine', and begged him to:

'remember the abundant flowing out and shedding of thy blood, which thou didst send out of thy body most plentifully, as out of grapes pressed at the wine-press, at such time as thou didst tread the winefat alone'.

Those words appeared in a *Book of Christian Prayers*, published in 1578, a copy of which belonged to Queen Elizabeth I; and they were said to be 'worthy to be read with an earnest mind of all Christians in these dangerous and troublesome days'.[4]

(iii)

It is early English literature which provides us with our second example of the cross and its message of judgement and hope. This is to be found in an Anglo-Saxon poem entitled *Christ*, the writer of which in dealing with the Last Judgement says:

'There sin-stained men in anguish of spirit
shall see as their fate the most fearful of woes:
It shall bring them no grace that the brightest of
    beacons,
The Rood of our Saviour red with his blood,
Over-run with bright gore, upreared before men,
With radiant light shall illumine the wide Creation.
No shadows shall lurk where the light of the Cross
Streams on all nations'.[5]

The inspiration for those lines was undoubtedly given by some words in the twenty-fourth chapter of the Gospel of

Matthew: 'Then shall appear the sign of the Son of man in heaven'.[6] From early days the Fathers and other Christian writers had understood this as being a reference to the cross of Christ towering over the world at the judgement. As to its actual form, none of them seems to have been quite sure: for while some visualised it simply as the wooden cross of Calvary, others saw it as the awe-inspiring cross which had appeared to Constantine. Nor did any of them develop the idea with such vivid imagination as that displayed by our own Anglo-Saxon poet. He too notes the marked contrast between sinful men who will gaze on the cross in anguish and fear, and the followers of the Crucified for whom it will be a sign of joy and hope.

It was the custom in pre-Reformation days on the feast of the Invention of the Cross, May 3, after the second lesson had been read at mattins, for everyone present to make the response: 'This sign of the cross will be in heaven when the Lord shall come in judgement'. Did one of those who joined in betray a slight shudder of fear? Might not that same fear be found even in some of us when we contemplate what are called the 'Last Things'?

To face death and judgement with some feelings of fear is not a sin. In the *Dream of Gerontius*, Newman makes the soul of Gerontius say to the angel shortly after death:

> 'Along my earthly life, the thought of death
> And judgement was to me most terrible.
> I had aye before me, and I saw
> The Judge severe e'en in the crucifix.
> Now that the hour is come, my fear is fled,
> And at this balance of my destiny,
> Now close upon me, I can forward look
> With a serenest joy'.

On the other hand, it is a great comfort to be without such fear, and to find in the cross what the old Latin hymn-writer calls our *spes unica:* 'one reliance'.[7]

(iv)

Our third example is a curious one which can be traced back to a verse in the First Letter of Peter in the New Testament. This tells of how after his death Christ 'went and preached to the spirits in prison, who formerly did not obey'.[8] However, for the full development of the idea of the descent to Hades and the setting up of the cross there we have to go to the apocryphal Gospel of Nicodemus. This provided the colourful material for what became known as the 'Harrowing of Hell' in both the liturgical drama which took place in church at the end of Holy Week, and in those medieval mystery plays performed each year in various English towns or cities by the trade guilds usually on the feast of Corpus Christi.

In the York Plays we find that it is the saddlers who are responsible for this lively and dramatic scene. They have to depict for their audience how Christ descends to Hades carrying with him the sign of the cross in order to redeem the departed souls and to bring them hope as he has already done for the men and women on earth. Artistic representations suggest that this cross would be in the form of what is known as the 'resurrection cross': that is a staff bearing a banner and having a cross at its end. It is with this standard that Christ breaks down the gates of Hades, shouting triumphantly as he does so, to the utter confusion of the demons and to the delight of human souls as also, without any doubt, to those who were watching the play:

'Undo your gates, ye princes of pride,
The king of bliss comes in this tide'.[9]

No less striking is an example of the depicting of the 'Harrowing of Hell' which comes from late Saxon times and is to be found carved on a seven-foot slab in Bristol Cathedral. Here Christ is shown as trampling with his feet on the beasts. In his right hand he has a cross; while with his left hand he

29

gives help and hope to a human soul struggling to be released.[10]

Obviously the so-called 'Harrowing of Hell' was of considerable interest to English writers, artists and sculptors in the Middle Ages. For us there lies behind it the important fact which is also indicated by the verse in the First Letter of Peter already mentioned, that our Lord's redemptive work was not limited to this earthly sphere but extended to that state of being which will one day be our own. Many Christians when they pray for those who have died are content to restrict their prayers to the 'faithful departed'. But surely there is a need to remind ourselves that our Lord gave his life on the cross for all mankind; and we ought to give careful thought to the suggestion contained in the recent report of the Archbishops' Commission *Prayers and the Departed* that we should associate ourselves with the divine purpose in commending also to God those who have died outside the faith of Christ.[11] For may not there be hope for them in the cross of Christ? And has not he himself shown us that the 'gates of Hades shall not prevail'?

(v)

The various symbols and the imagery referred to in this chapter to illustrate the cross and its message of both judgement and hope may not have the same appeal for us today as they had for our predecessors. In spite of this we should not allow ourselves to reject the important truths which lie behind them.

Moreover, there is one symbol in our land which still speaks as clearly as it has spoken for more than twelve hundred years; and that is the lovely Saxon cross of Bewcastle with its four sides decorated either by human figures, animals or birds, or by vine-scrolls with grapes and foliage, all of which were designed to convey to the faithful essentially Christian teaching. In order to find it one must go to a lonely spot amidst the rolling uplands of Cumberland, where once the

Romans had an outpost fort and where their soldiers may well have discussed the new faith to which the emperor Constantine had given his allegiance, little realising that the Roman altar [12] erected on this very spot to the local god Cocidius by the commander of the garrison perhaps a century earlier would one day be replaced by a great Christian cross.

If we search the records of the Bewcastle cross we shall discover something of its chequered history. Puritan fanaticism in the seventeenth century is alleged to have been responsible for the destruction of its cross-piece, so that all that now remains is the upright shaft. In later times, well-meaning antiquarians did the cross no good in their efforts to clean and examine the carvings and the runic inscriptions engraved on it. Even more recently, further damage was caused in the attempt to make a cast of it. Unlike its sister cross at Ruthwell a few miles away across the Scottish border, this cross has never been moved from its original position to a place of shelter, and so has been exposed to all the violent storms of wind and rain which sweep across these bleak moorlands.

Yet the Bewcastle cross, weather-worn though it is, still stands where it has stood for so long as a witness to the Christian faith in this land. More than that, there is upon the west face of its shaft the most perfectly carved figure of Christ. If he is the Christ in judgement trampling with his feet on two beasts, he is also the Christ of hope holding in one hand a scroll representing the Book of Life and raising his other hand in blessing.

There surely is a parable: for nothing could proclaim more clearly the message of hope than this wonderful old cross with the figure of Christ still visible upon it. It is that hope which can endure regardless of whatever men may do to us, and in spite of all the changes and chances of this earthly life.

NOTES

[1] E. T. Long, *Wall Paintings at Turvey and Wymington (Burlington Magazine*, lxviii, 1936, pp. 96–101).

[2] J. Boswell, *Life of Samuel Johnson,* 12 June 1784.

[3] C. Brown (ed.), *Religious Lyrics of the Fourteenth Century* (O.U.P. 1952), No. 25.

[4] W. K. Clay (ed.), *Private Prayers put forward during the reign of Queen Elizabeth* (Parker Society 1851), p. 512.

[5] C. W. Kennedy, *Early English Christian Poetry* (Hollis & Carter, 1952), p. 274.

[6] Matt. 24 : 30.

[7] *English Hymnal* No. 94, v. 6.

[8] I Pet. 3 : 19–20.

[9] J. S. Purvis (ed.), *The York Cycle of Mystery Plays* (S.P.C.K. 1957), p. 305.

[10] D. Talbot Rice, *English Art 871–1100* (O.U.P. 1952), p. 96.

[11] Report of the Archbishops' Commission on Christian Doctrine, *Prayer and the Departed* (S.P.C.K. 1971), pp. 53–5.

[12] F. Haverfield, *Roman Altar at Bewcastle* (*Transactions of the Cumberland and Westmorland Antiquarian and Archaeological Society,* vol. xv, 1899, p. 459).

III

RENUNCIATION

(i)

ABOUT eight miles off the coast of County Kerry in south-west Ireland there lies a rocky islet projecting out of the Atlantic ocean and known as Skellig Michael. It is difficult to imagine a wilder or more inaccessible place for human habitation. Even now it is only possible to land there in the calmest of seas. One of my most treasured and lasting memories will be of a day some years ago when, after waiting for nearly a whole week on account of bad weather, we were at last able to put in by boat at its landing-stage and then to climb the six hundred steps cut in the rock in order to reach its summit; and having got to the top, to see the remains of a small monastic community established there as long ago as the sixth or seventh century.[1]

There are the half-a-dozen bee-hive shaped cells 'clinging like swallows' nests' to the rock, originally inhabited by the monks; the two small oratories where once men prayed; a couple of wells which supplied the precious water; the ruins of a church with its altar on which the devout visitor still leaves a small offering; a tiny cemetery with grave-stones bearing incised crosses; and right in the centre of the main enclosure a crudely-shaped cross slab. Crudely-shaped it may have been, but that rough cross on the summit of Skellig Michael was to me deeply impressive and moving; for few things have ever brought home as that did the message of the cross and renunciation. Even though it would be more accurate historically to describe Skellig Michael as an example of Celtic rather than of Anglo-Saxon devotion to the cross, yet it may be that a monk from England occasionally found his way to that holy place, since Ireland was then renowned

33

for its learning, and English monks frequently took the opportunity of visiting it in order to partake of its culture.

The cross has always been at the very centre of the lives of those men and women who have experienced the call to serve as members of the religious orders. The nun, says the *Ancrene Riwle,* a medieval rule which was specially drawn up for the guidance of three English young ladies who had dedicated themselves to a life of prayer and renunciation, 'must see that she has the crucifix in the nest of her monastery and contemplate it often'.[2]

In the early part of this century a distinguished Protestant theologian from Germany, during his stay in England, asked if he might be allowed to visit one of the Anglican religious communities. There he had an opportunity of seeing for himself the simple but ordered way of life of its members; he shared for a brief space in its atmosphere of prayer and quiet; and ever before him he saw what was the motivating force behind it all, the cross of Christ. When, at the end, his companion asked him what were his impressions, the man replied with deep emotion: 'For every great movement to be a success, there must be some people who are willing to give the whole of themselves to it'.

(ii)

Jesus said, 'If any man would come after me, let him deny himself and take up his cross and follow me'.[3] Literally, this meant that the follower of Christ had to be ready to take the crossbeam on his shoulder, and to face the shame and the jeers of the crowd as he went forth to the place of execution. In its original setting in the Gospel of Mark, which was written at the time of the emperor Nero's persecution of the Church, that saying was undoubtedly intended to give the early Christians strength and encouragement in their hour of trial. They needed it: for the Roman historian, Tacitus, declares that they were regarded as the enemies of mankind; and like their Master many of them suffered a horrible death by crucifixion.

In the Gospel of Luke, written after the ending of the Neronian persecution when the circumstances had altered, the saying appears in a slightly different form: 'If any man would come after me, let him deny himself and take up his cross *daily* and follow me'.[4] There is however no weakening as regards the duty of renunciation on the part of the Christian disciple and his willingness to give up everything for his Master. Only later was it changed from its original meaning and given a purely moralising sense: so that there is a tendency now to describe all sorts of petty trials and tribulations as being part of 'our cross'.

Even John Wesley in preaching a sermon on self-denial on Luke's text, seems to adopt the conventional line when he says:

'A cross is anything contrary to our will, anything displeasing to our nature: so that taking up our cross goes a little farther than denying ourselves; it rises a little higher, and is a more difficult task to flesh and blood; it being more easy to forgo pleasure than to endure pain'.[5] While this is quite true, it ought never to be forgotten that real self-denial and the taking up of the cross means the renunciation of both reputation and life for Christ—nothing less than this.

In the eyes of the world, those early Christian martyrs suffering death on crosses in the arena of Rome, those sixth or seventh century monks enduring loneliness and hardships out there in the Atlantic on the rocky islet of Skellig Michael, and those members of the various orders voluntarily sacrificing their liberty and their possessions have all been fools. Each of them in turn would agree with that verdict: only they would add 'fools for Christ's sake'. Indeed in a book which seems to have been written for the fifteenth century Benedictine nuns of Chester, such readiness to be regarded as a fool for Christ is actually urged in the prayer:

'O Jesu let me never forget thy bitter passion
That thou sufferedst for my transgression
For in thy blessed wounds is the very school

That must teach me with the world to be called a fool'.[6]

Christ's followers, as long as they have been faithful to their Master, have never failed to recognise the duty of self-denial and renunciation. Twentieth century society provides us with ample opportunities for exercising our responsibility here, and for showing to the world that in the words of St. Paul we have been 'crucified with Christ', and that it is now Christ who dwells in us and who has replaced self as the centre of our lives.

(iii)

In the religious intolerance of seventeenth century England many devout men were called upon to deny themselves and take up the cross. There was, for example, the Anglican Jeremy Taylor, who out of his suffering produced those great spiritual classics *Holy Living* and *Holy Dying* which have been of guidance and inspiration to many people. There was the Quaker William Penn, the first edition of whose book *No Cross: No Crown* was set down in a prison cell, and which by its very title points the way to self-sacrifice. There was the Baptist John Bunyan, who during his twelve years in a Bedford gaol wrote *The Pilgrim's Progress*, one of the best-known books in the English language.

These were three men, each of whom remained loyal to his religious convictions and each of whom because of that loyalty was forced to bear the cross of renunciation. Jeremy Taylor suffered the loss of his benefice and was three times imprisoned by the Puritans on account of his Anglican principles. William Penn was locked up for nearly a year in the Tower of London, simply because he was a Quaker, and as such had refused to acknowledge himself guilty for having published a tract without first obtaining the required licence. John Bunyan as a Nonconformist was brought to trial and thrown into gaol under the penal laws of the Restoration period merely because he refused to give up his preaching.

Writing on what for some of us is a very real act of self-denial, Jeremy Taylor says: 'Be content to want praise; never be troubled when thou art slighted or undervalued'. William Penn asks the question as to what is the cross we should suffer, and gives the reply: 'The denying and offering up of ourselves to do or suffer the will of God for his service and glory'. John Bunyan in his immortal allegory tells us plainly what a Christian must be prepared to undergo once he has become obedient to the call of renunciation and has brought his burden to the cross.

It is painful to have to compare with men of this calibre some of the so-called religious leaders of the England of a century later: the kind of clergy of whom Jane Austen wrote in her novels. Here were men who chose to be ordained not with any thought of renunciation in their minds, but either to comply with the wishes of their parents, or because the Church seemed to them preferable to a career in the Army. Henry Gunning in his nineteenth century *Reminiscences of Cambridge* gives us a glimpse of just one of them. This was a Suffolk parson whose outstanding attractions were, first that he kept an excellent hunter, rode well up to the hounds and drank very hard, and was therefore much sought after by the country gentlemen; and secondly, that he sang an excellent song and danced so remarkably well that the young ladies considered no party was complete without his company.[7]

There was nothing whatever in that man's ministry of self-denial, and not the slightest thought of taking up the cross and following Christ. The very fact that we today are immediately revolted by such an example is an indication that we have come to expect, and rightly so, that the life of every priest should reflect something of the cross of renunciation.

(iv)

It is to the pioneers of the Oxford Movement of last century that the credit is largely due for setting members of the

Anglican Church on a new quest for holiness particularly in the matter of self-denial and renunciation. Thus, in the eyes of one of the movement's leaders, Dr. E. B. Pusey, the cross of Christ changed everything that it touched; it made weakness strength, sorrow joy, fasting a feast, and petty self-denials angelic crowns.[8]

Perhaps the idea of the cross as being mirrored and present in every act of self-denial on the part of the Christian disciple is nowhere better expressed than in one of the sermons of another, though lesser-known, Tractarian leader, Isaac Williams, where he says:

'The mystery of the cross has passed into every duty. . . . Every duty is a denial of self and therefore a bearing of the cross. And as the image of Christ crucified passes into all things that are his, like the sun in the heavens infinitely multiplying itself in all things, even the most insignificant on which it looks, so does this great law pass into all Christian duties, even the smallest of daily occurrence. . . . Rise early to prayer and it may be that it is an hour that has pain, but it has sweetness also for it has the image of the cross upon it, the pain of the reluctant flesh and sweetness of divine love.' [9]

The Tractarian or, as they became known later, Anglo-Catholic clergy had to learn the bitter lesson of the cross of self-denial and renunciation. Simply to express the intention of establishing the daily offices of Mattins and Evensong if one were to be appointed to a vacant benefice was sometimes sufficient to ensure that another person would be appointed as the new incumbent.[10] Many of them devoted their lives to serving slum parishes where some of the worst living conditions in England were to be found; and in return they were persecuted by hostile mobs, they were insulted by bishops, and they were left to carry on to the end of their days without any hope of change or preferment. Once more, as in pre-Reformation times, the cross was given its place on the altars of their churches, and the great rood once again hung high above the chancel; but for the priests themselves it was the cross of renunciation. They discovered for themselves:

'How all things are one great oblation made:
He on our altars, we on the world's rood'.

Such renunciation was only made possible because they
had come to accept a rigid discipline and self-denial in all
things in life. A letter of spiritual counsel written by John
Keble, another of the pioneers of the Oxford Movement and
one of the holiest of those associated with it, brings this out
very plainly:

'In the matter of self-denial, I may mention that perhaps
your studies of various kinds may give you room for some
exercise of the kind: you may set yourself a strict rule to
break off what you are about, though it be never so interesting—when the time comes for religious exercise. I think it
was John Wesley who set himself and others such strict rules
against the "lust of finishing".' [11]

Disciple of this kind may prove hard for some of us; but
then that surely is part of the content of self-denial and
renunciation.

'Self-denial', 'renunciation', and 'holiness' are not terms
which are as commonly heard now as they once were. Yet
without a vocabulary of that kind can one really understand
the full meaning of the cross and Christian discipleship? And
without the cross can one really greet others in the words with
which John Keble greeted his friend at the end of the letter
just quoted: 'A happy Easter'?

(v)

All who are familiar with the life of the early Church will
be well aware of the importance of renunciation for Christians
of those days. The fact that they had received the sign of the
cross in baptism and had thereby publicly renounced the
devil, the world and the flesh, meant a complete break with
their former associations and way of living. Only too often
this led to estrangement from families and friends; it entailed

the taking of a definite stand against many of the pleasures enjoyed by the members of a pagan society, and it could even involve the sacrificing of one's particular job of work. But then, after all, this was recognised as being a part of their discipleship as those early Christians were never allowed to forget. Woe betide them if they were thought to be too accommodating in the matter of worldly standards! Few could be more scathing in their denunciation of any such compromise than writers like Tertullian and Clement of Alexandria.

It is perhaps not without its point that in these days when renunciation and self-denial appear to be of diminishing importance the Church itself should once again be making renewed efforts to impress upon its members their responsibilities of giving a faithful witness in this connection. For example, in the Series II Baptismal service the parents and sponsors acting on behalf of the child to be baptised, through the affirmations which they make leave no doubt in the minds of the congregation that he or she who is about to receive the sign of the cross fully accepts the self-denial and renunciation which this implies. 'Do you turn to Christ?' is the first question put to them: to which there comes the reply 'I turn to Christ'. 'Do you renounce evil?' they are asked: to which the answer is given 'I renounce evil'.

For many Anglicans too the Easter Vigil, with those ancient and impressive ceremonies attached to it, has in recent years become more meaningful. One of the most welcome and challenging parts of the Vigil service, and one which should commend itself to every Christian whatever his particular shade of churchmanship, is the renewal of the baptismal vows. Here the priest first reminds his people of the New Testament teaching that their old self has been crucified with Christ, and that therefore they are no longer enslaved by sin; through Christ they are dead to sin but alive to God. He then calls on them to renew the promises made in their baptism, and he solemnly puts to them the question as to whether they renounce the devil and his works, the pomp and glory of the world, and all the sinful desires of the flesh. To this there comes the great response: 'We renounce them all'.

In such ways the duty of renunciation is again and again being brought home to Christians of today, and they are being made to realise the truth that: 'Christianity can never be merely a pleasant or consoling religion. It is a stern business. It is concerned with the salvation through sacrifice and love of a world in which as we can all see now, evil and cruelty are rampant. Its supreme symbol is the Crucifix—the total and loving self-giving of man to the redeeming purposes of God.' [12]

What that great mystic and spiritual writer of the first half of the twentieth century Evelyn Underhill sought to convey in those words which she wrote in her last letter, one of the outstanding architects of the second half of the century has endeavoured to illustrate by means of external symbolism. In the course of planning the new cathedral of Coventry, Sir Basil Spence was faced with the task of providing a chapel for private prayer with a screen before it to set it apart from the rest of the building. For this chapel, known as the Gethsemane Chapel, he designed a screen with the crown of thorns as the central motif. In this he was truly inspired: for there could be no better way of reminding all who go there to pray, that peace and tranquillity of mind are most surely to be found in self-sacrifice and renunciation.[13]

NOTES

[1] M. and L. de Paor, *Early Christian Ireland* (Thames & Hudson, 1958), pp. 52–6.

[2] F. A. Gasquet, *The Nun's Rule* (Chatto & Windus, 1926), p. 103.

[3] Mark 8: 34.

[4] Luke 9:23.

[5] E. H. Sugden (ed.), *Wesley's Standard Sermons* (Epworth, 1921), vol. ii, No. 42.

[6] J. W. Legg, *The Processional of the Nuns of Chester* (Henry Bradshaw Society, vol. xviii, p. 28).

[7] H. Gunning, *Reminiscences of Cambridge* (Bell, 1854), vol. ii, p. 63.

[8] E. B. Pusey, *Sermons during the Season from Advent to Whitsuntide* (Parker, 1848), p. 152.

[9] I. Williams, *Sermons preached in St. Saviour's Church, Leeds* (Parker, 1877), p. 163.

[10] S. L. Ollard, *A Short History of the Oxford Movement* (Faith Press Reprints, 1963), p. 143.

[11] J. Keble, *Letters of Spiritual Counsel* (Parker, 1885), p. 195.

[12] G. McLeod Bryan, *In His Likeness* (S.P.C.K., 1961), p. 173.

[13] B. Spence, *Phoenix at Coventry* (Bles, 1962), p. 101.

IV

LOVE

(i)

THERE lived in the city of Norwich during the fourteenth century one of the greatest of medieval English mystics. Her name was Juliana, but she is better known as Mother Julian or the Lady Julian of Norwich. Among the things which she had asked of God in her prayers was one which few women would be likely to request of him today: namely, that she might be allowed to have a vision of Christ in his Passion in order that she might gain a better understanding of it, and might suffer with both him and his Mother.

This unusual request was granted to Julian during a severe illness in her thirty-first year of age when those around her thought she was dying. Accordingly they sent for a priest so that he might be with her at the end; and he duly arrived bringing a crucifix which he set before her eyes.

It was in the hours which followed that Julian experienced those revelations which she later on so carefully set down in writing for all to read. There is nothing particularly novel in the message which she received: only in the circumstances of its delivery, and above all in the fact that this 'simple creature, unlettered', as she describes herself, should have proved to be such a source of inspiration to future generations. There is indeed more than enough material for Lenten reading and meditation in Julian's *Revelations of Divine Love* alone.

Her book is centred on the divine love as revealed to her in the cross. As she gazed on this she realised the depth of a love which willingly chose that cross and patiently suffered upon it; and she became aware that the love which made him suffer surpassed all his pain so far as heaven is above earth. She saw Christ's love for her revealed in his wondrous side; and again in the sight of his love for his Mother even while he

43

endured his sufferings on the cross. She was also comforted by the revelation that neither pain nor sorrow could separate her from the love of Christ.

Finally, when some fifteen years later, once more restored to health and living the life of a recluse in a little cell close to her church just outside Norwich, Julian pondered over her experience and sought to understand its purpose and meaning, the answer suddenly came to her:

'Wouldst thou learn thy Lord's meaning in this thing? Learn it well: Love was his meaning. Who showed it thee? Love. What showed he thee? Love. Wherefore showed it he? For Love. Hold thee therein and thou shalt learn and know more in the same'.[1] In this way, she says, she learned that love was the meaning of the cross.

She was perfectly right, because if there is one thing which shines out from the cross it is the divine love. Jesus himself says: 'Greater love has no man than this that a man lay down his life for his friends'; Paul speaks of 'the Son of God who loved me and gave himself for me'; and the writer of the closing book of the New Testament, the Revelation of John, refers in a great outburst of praise, to 'him who loved us and has freed us from our sins by his blood'.

(ii)

Perhaps more than any others it was the Franciscan friars who brought home to the men and women of medieval England the full meaning of the love of Christ as proclaimed through the cross, both by their example and their message. Following the way of life of their founder Francis of Assisi, they chose for their homes the most wretched places they could find: the name 'Stinking Lane', the site of their London house, is in itself sufficiently descriptive. In having their dwellings with the poorest and the outcasts of society they showed something of the love that was to be seen in the lowly stable of Bethlehem and on the cross of Calvary.

The Franciscans asked what should be man's response to

the divine love. And the answer they gave was: all of which he is capable. It is summed up in the words so frequently used by Francis himself: 'Deus meus et omnia': 'My God and my all'. Although separated both in time and in theological outlook from the English nonconformist divine and hymn-writer Isaac Watts, they would have been at one with him when he wrote:

'Love so amazing, so divine,
Demands my soul, my life, my all'.

The love of human beings for Christ as it might and ought to be was surely never more touchingly illustrated than in a poem written by a thirteenth century Franciscan who later became Archbishop of Canterbury, John Pecham. He was born at Patcham in Sussex and so would have known and perhaps often have gazed on the splendid wall-paintings in the nearby church of Clayton, then fresh from the artist's brush, with the four angels bearing a cross and other angels holding instruments of the passion, and the great figure of Christ towering above all.

Pecham called his poem *Philomena,* a word which means 'nightingale', because this bird plays such an important part in it. The poem recounts the legend of the nightingale who, when near to death, is supposed to fly to the top of a tree at day-break, and there to sing its song with ever-growing passion and intensity, until at last as the shadows of evening lengthen, it becomes utterly exhausted and falls dying to the ground. In that small bird he saw a representative of the human soul which is overflowing with love for Christ. Just as the nightingale sang through the day, so the devout soul is portrayed by the poet as following in meditation hour by hour the earthly life of Christ, until at the ninth hour, that life is given up in death on the cross.

'Then the soul, as if distraught, cries repeatedly:
"Let the executioners come and fasten me
Christ, with thee upon thy cross; sweet my lot would be,
If I might, in such a way, die embracing thee".' [2]

45

Such was the unique and attractive method employed by an English Franciscan in endeavouring to win the love of his fellow-countrymen for their Saviour. To Pecham we are also indebted for a splendid phrase which conveys to us both the idea of Christ as a friend which became a popular one in later English medieval thought, and also the archbishop's own sense of the divine love and generosity in man's redemption and what should be our response: 'I say he has loved courteously, expecting no return'.[3]

(iii)

Christ through his death on the cross calls men to give their love not only to himself but to others as well. When, long centuries ago, the pagans were masters of this island, they made much of certain ideals such as the ideal of heroism. But it was left to Christianity to bring with it the ideals of love and tenderness, and so, incidentally, to give a new status to women. One is made to realise this when one looks at the Saxon cross of Ruthwell and discovers that no less than four out of its ten panels have scenes in which women play a part. Before the coming of the Christian faith to Britain anything of this kind on a public monument would have been unthinkable: it was the love of Christ which was responsible for the change.

If we were asked to select one particular episode from the Gospels as demonstrating Christ's love and tenderness for others, especially women, we might very well choose that incident recorded in the passion narrative of the Fourth Gospel, where as he hung on the cross in his last hours, Jesus commended to his friend and disciple John the one whom he loved best of all: his Mother, our Lady Mary.

People in the Middle Ages, like Margery Kempe of King's Lynn in Norfolk, had 'great wonder how our Lady might suffer or endure to see his precious body be scourged and hanged on the cross'.[4] As they pondered over it, they came to feel an intense love and devotion for Mary in her anguish and sorrow. Poems and passion carols began to be composed around this theme. Some of them took the form of a dialogue between Jesus as he hung on the cross and his Mother as she stood beneath it, such as this one which begins:

> 'Mother, stand firm beneath the Rood!
> Look on your Son in cheerful mood;
> Joyful, Mother, should you be'.

> 'Son, how should I joyful stand?
> I see your foot, I see your hand
> Nailed upon the cruel tree.' [5]

How should, or could she indeed?

A preacher of the early fifteenth century in a sermon on the passion, drew a vivid picture of the contrast between on the one hand Nazareth and Bethlehem and on the other Calvary, as it must have seemed to Mary standing beside the cross. Whereas in those days which seemed so long ago, the angel had promised that Christ would be her son, now she had to accept the loss of him and the gift of another 'son' in his place; whereas then the angel had told her that the fruit of her womb would be blessed, now she had to look upon Jesus as one cursed; whereas then she had heard the angels singing, now she saw his friends weeping; and whereas then kings and shepherds had paid him homage and worship, now she had to watch men of every sort treating him with spite and cruelty.[6]

Nevertheless, even though she was undergoing such bitter anguish, Mary *stood;* and the quiet dignity and self-control which the Gospel attributes to our Lady in those hours of grief and in the depth of her love for her Son, is in striking contrast to the way in which some of the later medieval writers portrayed her, as raging hysterically, tearing her hair, swooning in the arms of John, and having to be carried from the scene.

Rather than indulge in fanciful exaggerations of this kind, let us recall the comment of Bishop Jeremy Taylor, so faithful to our Anglican tradition that 'though her grief was great enough to swallow her up, yet her love was greater, and did swallow up her grief';[7] and let us leave the Blessed Virgin keeping her vigil beside the cross as the sun disappears behind it, with the words of a beautiful thirteenth century English lyric, which has been called 'Sunset on Calvary':

> 'Now sinks the sun beneath the wood
> Mary I pity your lovely face;
> Now sinks the sun beneath the Rood
> Mary, I pity your Son and you'.[8]

(iv)

When Jesus hung on the cross he was offered the customary drink of strong wine mixed with myrrh specially prepared in order to ease the sufferings of those who were crucified. The responsibility of looking after this appears to have rested entirely with some of the women of Jerusalem. They provided it at their own expense and without any reward; it was an act of mercy and love.

All of us Christians nowadays are continually being made aware of our responsibilities in the matter of love and care for other people. From the emphasis which is laid on it one might at times almost imagine that this was some new teaching. In fact it stems from the Founder of Christianity, Jesus himself, who having forced from a highly respectable man the somewhat grudging recognition of acts of mercy done by an outcast member of society immediately urged the man to go and do likewise.

The medieval Church reminded its members of their obligations in this respect by setting down as a guide, though it is by no means to be regarded as exclusive, what have ever since been known as the seven Works of Mercy. These are: to feed the hungry, to give drink to the thirsty, to clothe the naked, to give shelter to the homeless, to visit the sick, to ransom the prisoner, and to bury the dead. In some of our parish churches the works of mercy are still to be seen either in stained glass windows or in wall-paintings; and they have found a place in the English devotional writers from Bede to the present day.

For many people in the second half of the twentieth century, especially those of the younger generation, it is this concern of Christianity with love and compassion that matters most. A recently published book went so far as to describe caring as 'the golden core of religion'. Even though a practising Christian is aware that there are other important elements in his religion besides this one, nevertheless caring must have a high place when we recall the teaching and example set by Jesus, who once said 'As you did it to one of the least of these my brethren, you did it to me';[9] and who, when he was suffering the most intense agony on the cross could still show love and compassion for others.

It is surely not without significance that in many of the hymns and carols produced in recent years, such as those of Sydney Carter, caring and the cross are both given a prominent place. The writer of a hymn in the lately published *100 Hymns for Today* puts into words the feelings of many of his contemporaries when he says:

> 'The groaning of creation,
> wrung out by pain and care.
> The anguish of a million hearts
> that break in dumb despair;
> O crucified Redeemer,
> these are thy cries of pain;
> O may they break our selfish hearts,
> and love come in to reign'.[10]

(v)

There is one other matter which cannot but force itself upon our attention as we contemplate the cross and love: and that is our relationship with fellow-Christians of other denominations. For all too long what the Book of Common Prayer describes as 'our unhappy divisions' have been a cause

D

of scandal; and the words 'See how these Christians love one another' which were originally used in wonder at a truly amazing fellowship, have only too often in later times been applied in irony to those torn apart by disunity and strife.

Now, at last, there is an ever-growing awareness of the great truth voiced centuries ago in the pages of *Piers Plowman*, that we are all blood-brothers at the cross of Christ. If we, divided as we are still, can meet anywhere, it is at the cross: because it is at the cross of Christ that Catholic devotion and Evangelical preaching unite. An Anglican leader gave expression to this when at a conference held as far back as the year 1925 he said:

'The nearer we draw to the Crucified, the nearer we come to one another, in however varied colours the Light of the World may be reflected in our faith. Under the cross of Jesus Christ we reach out hands to one another. The Good Shepherd had to die in order that he might gather together the scattered children of God. In the crucified and risen Lord alone lies the world's hope.' [11]

When, for example, Christians of differing traditions are called to undergo suffering or persecution together, when, like the late Bishop Leonard Wilson in those terrible days in Singapore during the Second World War, one finds oneself in a prison which is so overcrowded that one cannot lie down and one has to be thankful for a few grains of burnt rice with which to be able to celebrate Holy Communion for one's fellow-prisoners, when in other words the Church is under the cross, then how unimportant seem the differences beside a common faith and hope in the one Christ. Or when again, Christians of various denominations are faced with some emergency and are called to share together in the task of relieving the starving or the homeless, or of assisting the victims of some natural disaster, the very fact of being united in the service of Christ and of working and praying together has the effect of minimising differences of theology.

The twentieth century ecumenical movement provides remarkable instances of the way in which what seemed not so many years ago to be totally insurmountable barriers have been broken down and overcome through Christian love. Many no doubt have been able to share in moving experiences of a kind which will always remain in their memories. For myself I can never forget the occasion when, in a little village church in France when I was far away from any Anglican ministrations, the parish priest not merely offered a welcome but also the opportunity of partaking in the sacrament of the Eucharist: and we, the ordained representatives of two great Churches which in the past have so often been bitterly divided, found ourselves one in Christ's sacrifice and Christ's love.

NOTES

[1] Julian of Norwich, *Revelations of Divine Love* (ed. G. Warrack), (Methuen, 1945), p. 202.

[2] J. Pecham, *Philomena* (trans. W. Dobell), (Burns & Oates, 1924).

[3] D. Douie, *Archbishop Pecham's Sermons and Collations* (in *Studies in Medieval History presented to Sir M. Powicke,* O.U.P., 1948, p. 277).

[4] W. Butler-Bowdon (ed.), *The Book of Margery Kempe* (World's Classics, O.U.P. 1954), p. 215.

[5] B. Stone (ed.), *Medieval English Verse* (Penguin, 1964), p. 195.

[6] G. R. Owst, *Literature and Pulpit in Medieval England,* p. 541.

[7] J. Taylor, *The Great Exemplar* (*Works,* ed. C. P. Eden, 1856, vol. ii, p. 710).

[8] C. Brown (ed.), *Religious Lyrics of the Thirteenth Century* (O.U.P., 1932), No. 24.

[9] Matt. 25:40.

[10] T. Rees, *Christ Crucified Today* (No. 71 in *100 Hymns for Today*), (William Clowes, 1969).

[11] S. Neill and R. Rouse, *A History of the Ecumenical Movement* (S.P.C.K., 1954), p. 548.

V

SUFFERING

(i)

WHEN the eleventh-century Archbishop of Canterbury, Anselm, in one of his *Prayers* cried out:

'Why, O my soul, were you not present to be transfixed with the sword of sharpest grief: at the unbearable sight of the spear piercing the side of your Saviour; at seeing those nails which tore the hands and feet of him who made you; at the horror of the pouring out of your Redeemer's blood',[1] he was giving expression to the growing awareness in his time of the physical sufferings of the crucified Christ.

The association of the cross with suffering has certainly exercised an important influence on both English religious thought and devotion. Christians in the earlier centuries of the Church's history, in contrast to ourselves today, found it very much easier to accept the divinity of Christ than his humanity. To them, Jesus reigned from the tree as the glorified divine Lord. Relatively little attention was paid to his sufferings as a man, in spite of the attempts of New Testament writers, particularly the author of the Fourth Gospel and of the First Letter of John, to correct what was obviously becoming a one-sided emphasis even before the end of the first century. A monk of Constantinople in the fifth century went so far as to declare that the humanity of Christ was absorbed by his divinity as a drop of water is swallowed up in the ocean. If that were really the case, his experience of human suffering would be meaningless; and the Church rightly, in its condemnation of this heresy, pointed out that there was no such confusion of the two natures in Christ's Person.

Then as time passed, the pendulum swung in the other

direction, as no one who compares the earliest crucifixes with those of the later Middle Ages can possibly fail to appreciate. The upright and serene figure of Christ reigning from the tree has given place to one with drooping head, bent body and eyes closed in death. 'It has ceased to be a symbol of the Word, and has become the pathetic image of the Son of Man',[2] expressive above all of human suffering.

Could anyone possibly fail to grasp the reality of the sufferings of Christ when they were set forth in such a manner as Anselm set them forth in his prayer; or when they were expounded so movingly as by the fourteenth century English Dominican friar, John Bromyard, in his *Summa praedicantium,* a book of 'Helps for preachers'? Dwelling on the fact of Christ as suffering in his five senses, Bromyard contrasts the head whose beauty is boundless with that crowned with thorns, and the face which angels desire to look upon with that spat on by unbelievers. He draws attention to those ears accustomed to hear the angelic song, now having to listen to human blasphemies; and to the feet and hands belonging to him who made the world being nailed to the cross. Finally, he reminds his readers how Christ suffers in his sense of taste from the vinegar which was given him to drink; and in his sight from beholding the grief of Mary his mother.[3]

(ii)

For the majority of men and women living in England during the Middle Ages life was at best a hard affair, with much of it being spent in evil-smelling streets, and in insanitary hovels which would nowadays be condemned by the R.S.P.C.A. as unfit for animals, and with the parish church as the only thing which brought light, beauty and colour into their drab lives. Added to this there was the unstable state of society, and the imminence of suffering and death brought about by wars and other disasters, above all by the dreadful mid-fourteenth century epidemic which is known to us as the Black Death.

An outbreak of plague was not a novel event to the people of England at that time; but the revolting nature of the Black Death which rendered its victims objects of disgust rather than of pity, their total inability to take any effective precautions or measures to counteract it, and the swiftness with which it could wipe out an entire community, all came as a terrible shock to those unfamiliar with twentieth century weapons of destruction which human beings have invented to achieve precisely the same effects.

Is it surprising then, that for these folk in their sufferings there should be an ever-growing concentration on the physical sufferings of Christ on the cross? Is it really so strange that preachers of sermons and writers of treatises and verses should tend to magnify his torments, and that artists and sculptors should portray the agonies of the figure on the crucifix in ever-increasing degrees of realism? So it was that Richard Rolle, a fourteenth century hermit and mystic of Hampole in Yorkshire, who died in the year 1349 and therefore may himself have been a victim of the Black Death, wrote in his *Meditations on the Passion* of Christ on the cross as being like heaven full of stars, or as a net or a dovecot full of holes, or as a honeycomb full of cells, so filled was his body with wounds.[4]

In a British Museum manuscript of the fifteenth century,[5] which has been attributed to a Carthusian monastery, there is a curious assortment of religious passages in verse and prose, accompanied by water-colour illustrations some of which show Christ's body as covered from head to foot with little red stains representing his wounds; one of them portrays a wounded heart with the words on it 'This is the measure of the wounds which Jesus Christ suffered for our redemption', and there is even an attempt made to set down in figures the exact number of the Saviour's wounds. So, too, in a few English parish churches there are still to be seen surviving examples of late medieval wall-paintings which leave no doubt in our minds as to the deep impression which they would have made on the people of the time as to the reality of Christ's suffering. Many a devout lay man or woman must have been moved by them to feel, as did Margery Kempe of King's Lynn, that Christ's death and passion were as fresh as if he died that same day, and that so it should be to all Christian people.[6] For all that, no English artist of the Middle Ages in his portrayal of the passion ever quite reached in horrifying details the work of Matthias Grünewald in the celebrated altar-piece at Colmar in Alsace.

Turning to the early years of the seventeenth century, one or two of the sermons of Bishop Lancelot Andrewes, preached before King James I, show the reality of Christ's sufferings for him. In a Good Friday sermon given at Whitehall in 1604, Andrewes says:

'Our very eye will soon tell us no place was left in his body where he might be smitten and was not: his skin and flesh rent with the whips and scourges; his hands and feet wounded with the nails; his head with the thorns, his very heart with the spear-point, all his senses, all his parts laden with whatever wit or malice could invent; his blessed body given as an anvil to be beaten upon'.[7] And in another Good Friday sermon preached at Greenwich in the following year, he says:

'They did not whip him, they ploughed his back and made long furrows upon it; they did not put on his wreath of thorns and press it down with their hands, but beat it on hard with bats to make it enter through skin, flesh, skull and all; they did not pierce his hands and feet, but made wide holes (like that of a spade) as if they had been digging in some ditch'.[8] Here we have what is almost the literary counterpart of Grünewald; and if such horrific descriptions should cause us to shudder today, at least they serve as a salutary reminder that the Christ who lived for thirty-three years in the world of men was not some remote and far-off figure unmoved by human affliction, but one who knew to the full what that suffering may mean.

(iii)

Among the short popular prayers dating from the later

Middle Ages, the sort of prayers which would have been used by countless numbers of simple and unlettered folk, either as they passed by a crucifix, or during service-time in church, or possibly before going to bed at night, there is one which focuses the attention on Christ's sufferings:

> 'Jesus Christ of Nazareth
> That for us all sufferedst death
> Upon the rood tree;
> Through virtue of your wounds five
> That you suffered in your life
> Have mercy on me'.[9]

It is a reference in that prayer which leads us to the consideration of something which seems to have meant much to Englishmen in their devotion to the passion: namely the five wounds of Christ: those imprints in his hands, his feet and his side.

The revival of the Religious Orders in the Middle Ages, with the Christo-centric piety of men like the Franciscans coupled with the enthusiasm of those returning home after serving as Crusaders in the Holy Land, appears to have marked the beginning of a special devotion for our Lord's five wounds.[10] People began to think of those wounded members of his human body as having endured special torments on their behalf; and they were led to reverence the wounds themselves as being the particular marks of Christ's love.

So it came about that prayers were composed which contained specific references to the wounds, and in due course a votive Mass of the Five Wounds became very popular. Furthermore, as can still be seen in some English churches there were various representations of the five wounds: as on a wooden bench-end at North Cadbury in Somerset, on a roof-boss in Winchester Cathedral, and on a stone shield in the University church at Oxford. Rich men left in their wills bequests of money to the poor in honour of the wounds of Christ. In the year 1536 those taking part in the Pilgrimage of Grace carried as their emblem a banner bearing on it the five wounds of the Saviour, and the same sign was embroidered on their sleeves. Many of our altars are still marked with five small crosses signifying the imprints of Christ's passion.

Nor is such devotion exclusively 'Catholic': for it was Charles Wesley who wrote in one of his hymns:

> 'Five bleeding wounds, he bears,
> Received on Calvary;
> They pour effectual prayers,
> They strongly speak for me:
> Forgive him, O forgive! they cry,
> Nor let that ransomed sinner die! '

Is not there here an echo of that which seems to have proved of such spiritual help to the people of medieval England: that is of the idea of the five wounds of our Lord as being various wells? So the wound in his right hand was regarded as the well of mercy, and that in his left hand as the well of grace; the wound in his right foot was seen as the well of pity, and that in his left foot as the well of comfort; while the wound in his side which became the object of the utmost veneration was seen as the well of life, and the water and blood which flowed from it came to be treated by some writers as symbolic of the sacraments of Baptism and the Eucharist.

The manuscript in the British Museum referred to earlier in this chapter contains an intricate drawing in which red lines representing Christ's blood proceed from his side as he hangs on the cross.[11] They extend over illustrations of the seven sacraments: to the forehead of a boy being baptised, and to that of a child receiving confirmation; to the hand of a priest joining two together in marriage, and to that of another pronouncing absolution; to the head of one receiving ordination; to the blessed sacrament upon an altar; and finally to the breast of a person being anointed. By this means all who studied the book would be made aware of the connection between the wound in the Saviour's side and the sacraments of his Church.

(iv)

'An indelible impression' is how we sometimes speak of the effects which some experience has left upon our being. In the case of Jesus, this seems to have been true in regard to the five wounds; for it is clear from the Gospels of Luke and John that those were marks which neither death nor even the resurrection were able to blot out. 'See my hands and feet, that it is I myself; handle me and see',[12] says the risen Christ to the bewildered and frightened eleven as they are gathered together. 'Put your finger here, and see my hands; and put out your hand, and place it in my side; do not be faithless, but believing',[13] he says to the incredulous Thomas. And Thomas, although rejoicing to see his Master, would also no doubt be a sadder and wiser man at such a sight as that of the wounds.

The fact of this particular impression should be of importance to Christians: for it is surely a reminder to us that the joy of our religion, such as the joy brought both by the incarnation and resurrection, can never be superficial. So far from that, Christian joy is something very deep in its quality; it is something which can never be oblivious to the existence of suffering.

A priest who knew this for himself, both in his life and death, and who therefore typifies so well the association between the cross and suffering in English life and devotion, was Austin Thompson sometime vicar of St. Peter's Eaton Square, in London. In his later years it became his custom to have placed among the white flowers which decorated the altar on Easter Day, one or two red blooms in order to symbolise the marks of the wounds in Christ's risen body. That custom is to me a pleasing one: because although in itself it appears to be a minor detail, yet it can be of help to some people in their devotion and bring home to them the deeper side of their Faith.

It was my own privilege to serve that devoted priest at the altar on the morning of what was to be his last Easter; because on the night of Wednesday in Easter week 1941, so soon after he had celebrated the joy of the resurrection, Austin Thompson, like the apostle, was to discover for himself the wound-prints in the body of his Master. In his anxiety for his people who were sheltering in the crypt of his church he courageously went out alone on to its steps during an air-raid to undertake the task of firewatching. Almost instantly he was struck down by a bomb, and thus was called to share in the sufferings of the risen Christ. His death was surely a fulfilment of the prayer:

> 'By thy Five Wounds, O Lord Christ . . .
> shew the triumph of faith,
> that we may believe,
> and do battle to the end'.[14]

(v)

The prayer of Anselm quoted at the beginning of this chapter, in which he expressed his awareness of the reality of the sufferings of the Crucified Christ, has found its echo in every period of our history since that time. Each generation has produced its representatives to develop the theme of Christ's sufferings on the cross in a manner most appropriate to their own situation and needs.

For some of our contemporary artists and poets the consciousness of belonging to a world which has experienced a major war, not to mention many 'minor' though no less ghastly conflicts, as well as the nightmare of nuclear weapons and concentration camps, and for a large percentage of the population the horrors of famine, poverty and starvation, is very real. It is hardly surprising therefore that for these painters and writers the representation of the crucified Christ by Matthias Grünewald in all its stark realism and agony should be the one which seems to have the strongest appeal and to speak best to this day and age.

The painting of the crucifixion by one of the foremost

artists of the twentieth century, Graham Sutherland, in the church of St. Matthew, Northampton, is the outstanding example of this tendency.[15] When in 1944, Sutherland was invited to paint for that church an Agony in the Garden he asked to be allowed to substitute for it one of the crucifixion. Then for many months he pondered over his subject. The imagery of thorns, and particularly of the crown of thorns which seemed to him to be the supreme instance of human cruelty towards Christ, again and again impressed itself both on his mind and his artist's canvas.

Sutherland knew at that time the Grünewald masterpiece only from seeing reproductions of it just as he knew of the sufferings of innocent men and women in the Nazi concentration camps only from hearing about them; but both these were enough to provide him with the inspiration for his own great work which he at last completed in 1946. There indeed do we see Christ as suffering in the suffering of his people. The immense cross, with the sagging figure on it whose shoulders are being torn by the very weight of the body itself, and, of course, the spiked thorns: all these create an impression of untold horror: a horror which is heightened by the fact that the traditional bystanders are absent and we ourselves take their place as witnesses of the scene.

Some of the poets of our time have also tried through the pattern of verse to convey a similar message. One, by means of the imagery of incessant rain which falls, as it has fallen for more than nineteen hundred years, on guilty and innocent alike, has sought to show how the sufferings of Calvary are seen again in the cruelties of modern warfare, causing the blood still to fall 'from the starved Man's wounded side'.[16] Another has compared the utter indifference of that crowd of 'ordinary decent folk' to what was being done on the first Good Friday 'as three pale figures were led forth and bound',[17] with that of ourselves, content as so many of us who call ourselves Christians are to stand by and watch acts of tyranny or cruelty without ever raising our voices in protest. Perhaps no one speaks more truly for us and our society than does David Gascoyne, when in the horrifying realism of his poem *Ecce Homo*, he says:

> 'He is in agony till the world's end,
> And we must never sleep during that time!
> He is suspended on the cross-tree now
> And we are onlookers at the crime,
> Callous contemporaries of the slow
> Torture of God. Here is the hill
> Made ghastly by his spattered blood
> Whereon he hangs and suffers still.' [18]

NOTES

[1] Anselm, *Opera omnia* (ed. F. S. Schmitt, Nelson, 1946–61, *Oratio 2*, vol. iii, p. 7).

[2] K. Clark, *The Nude* (Pelican, 1960), p. 223.

[3] R. Woolf, *The English Religious Lyric in the Middle Ages* (O.U.P., 1968), p. 223.

[4] H. E. Allen (ed.), *English Writings of Richard Rolle* (O.U.P., 1931), pp. 34–5.

[5] Brit. Mus. Add. Ms. 37049.

[6] W. Butler-Bowdon, *The Book of Margery Kempe*, p. 193.

[7] L. Andrewes, *XCVI Sermons* (1661), p. 353.

[8] ibid., p. 374.

[9] R. H. Robbins, *Popular Prayers in Middle English Verse* (Modern Philology, vol. 36, 1939).

[10] On the Five Wounds, *Notes and Queries*, N.S. x. 1963, pp. 50, 82, 127, 163.

[11] Brit. Mus. Add. Ms. 37049, fol. 72vo. and fol. 73. Also, F. Wormald, *Some popular miniatures and their rich relations* (in *Miscellanea pro arte, Festschrift für Hermann Schnitzler*, Dusseldorf, 1967, pp. 279–285).

[12] Luke 24 : 39.

[13] John 20 : 27.

[14] E. Milner White, *A Procession of Passion Prayers* (S.P.C.K., 1952), p. 122.

[15] D. Cooper, *The Work of Graham Sutherland* (Lund, Humphries, 1961).

[16] E. Sitwell, *Still Falls the Rain* (in *The Song of the Cold* Macmillan, 1945, p. 15).

[17] W. H. Auden, *The Shield of Achilles* (Faber, 1955).

[18] D. Gascoyne, *Collected Poems* (O.U.P., 1965), p. 44.

VI

PENITENCE

(i)

ONE of the most interesting of the panels carved on the celebrated Anglo-Saxon cross at Ruthwell in Dumfriesshire where
the influence of Northumbria then made itself felt, depicts
our Lord with the woman who was a sinner. At the feet of an
exceedingly fine figure of Christ, who is shown as draped in
a long robe and having his right hand raised in an attitude of
pardon and blessing, there kneels Mary Magdalene. In front
of her is what looks like her arm but in fact is a great mass
of hair with which she wipes the Saviour's feet so lately made
wet with her penitential tears. Lest anyone should fail to
recognise the scene and its message, the sculptor has filled the
margin around it with the Latin text of the incident as recorded
in Luke's Gospel.

Experts on the Ruthwell Cross, while admiring the balance
in which this scene has been portrayed, are no less amazed at
the crudeness of the figure of Mary Magdalene, particularly
the awkwardness of her arm and hand, and the contrast
between this and the supreme craftsmanship of the figure of
Christ. So marked is the difference that some of them are
forced to the conclusion that when the master craftsman had
completed the Christ he left it to the hand of another, possibly
one of his pupils, to finish off the work.

For us, however, the main value of that panel on the cross
of Ruthwell is its reminder of the association of the cross in
English life and devotion with penitence. Whoever the
sculptor may have been, and whatever the theme of his
carvings, he was anxious that those who came to gaze on his
great sermon in stone should have this episode of human
penitence and divine forgiveness ever before their eyes.

It is Luke who more than any of the writers of our New Testament Gospels lays stress on the forgiveness of Christ, both in his record of this incident and above all in his narrative of the passion where he alone records the Saviour's prayer 'Father, forgive them' and the episode of the penitent thief. But to know the forgiveness of Christ we must first, like the woman who was a sinner, come to him in faith and penitence; we must be aware of the measure of our sin, as was St. Anselm when, in one of his *Meditations,* he cried out:

'I myself am the wound of your sorrow, I am to blame for your murder. I have merited that you should die. I am the scourge of vengeance upon you. I am the real malice in your passion, the real suffering in your crucifixion',[1] and we must pray in the words of an ancient collect that we may be enabled 'so to feel and understand that we may have true repentance and good perseverance all the days of our life'.[2]

(ii)

Not very long after the setting up of the Ruthwell cross the people of England were given another reminder of the call to penitence when, in the Good Friday Liturgy during the Veneration of the Cross, they heard for the first time those touching remonstrances known as the Reproaches. If you have ever heard them particularly in the Palestrina setting, as I heard them sung in St. Peter's in Rome as Pope John XXIII, pale and dying, led the faithful in their solemn adoration of that on which the Lord was crucified, you will know how deeply moving they can be.

Words from the Old Testament prophet Micah form the opening sentence in a set of reproaches which Jesus is represented as uttering against his own people on account of their treatment of him. Here is the English version of them as they appeared in the Sarum or Salisbury use so familiar to our countrymen in days before the Reformation:

'O my people, what have I done unto thee, or wherein have I wearied thee? testify against me. Because I brought thee up out of the land of Egypt, thou hast prepared a cross for thy Saviour.'

'Because I led thee through the wilderness forty years, and fed thee with manna, and brought thee into a land sufficiently good, thou hast prepared a cross for thy Saviour.'

'What could I have done more unto thee that I have not done? I planted thee indeed, O my vineyard, with fair fruit, and thou art become very bitter unto me; for thou gavest me to drink in my thirst vinegar mingled with gall, and piercedst thy Saviour's side with a spear.' As one listens to such a recital what more fitting response could there be than the deep and heartfelt cries: 'Holy God, Holy and Strong, Holy and Immortal, have mercy upon us'?

Early in the reign of Edward VI that impressive Good Friday ceremony known to Englishmen as 'creeping to the cross' was abolished, and with it the liturgical use of the Reproaches. But it could well be that in the following century, during the Laudian era when fine music was once again to be heard in many of our cathedrals and churches that the devout Anglican priest, George Herbert, was able to listen to those verses in one or other of their settings on the occasions when he attended service in Salisbury Cathedral or else in the music meetings which were held afterwards. That however was the limit, and they were, of course, entirely removed from their liturgical context. For the people of his small country parish of Bemerton, Herbert had to be content to write a poem which he called *The Sacrifice*. Beginning as this does with the words 'O all ye who pass by', and having as the concluding refrain at the end of almost every verse the lament 'Was ever grief like mine', there is a strong possibility that the liturgical material used in the medieval Church on the last three days of Holy Week, and in particular the Reproaches, formed its basis and inspiration.[3]

Today, with the growing desire for enrichment in our Holy Week liturgy and worship, there is a widespread restoration of the former Good Friday service, which incidentally many Anglicans, following the phraseology of the Taizé community,

would probably prefer to call 'The Adoration of the Crucified'; and with it of the recitation of those ancient verses so
evocative to penitence, the Reproaches.

(iii)

In the closing verses of his Gospel, Luke refers to the risen
Christ as charging his disciples 'that repentance and forgiveness of sins should be preached in his name to all nations'.[4]
Hence the apostle Peter, in the earliest Christian preaching
recorded in the Acts of the Apostles, after reminding his
audience that they were responsible for sending Christ to the
cross goes on to urge the need for their repentance in the
words: 'Repent and be baptised every one of you in the name
of Jesus Christ for the forgiveness of your sins'.[5]
Throughout history those proclaiming the Christian gospel
have been obedient to this charge and pattern. Their task has
never been an easy one; and perhaps in England it has been
even harder than elsewhere. For we must not forget that in all
probability it was in this island that in the fourth century
Pelagius was born: and the Pelagian doctrine of man's self-
sufficiency and his independence of God's grace, with its con-
sequent denial of the necessity of the redemptive work of
Christ on the cross and its tendency towards complacency and
smugness, has always had a peculiar attraction for Englishmen.

Accordingly, preachers and writers in medieval England
had no hesitation in resorting to the method adopted in the
Good Friday reproaches: namely of endeavouring to move
people to penitence by representing Christ himself as appealing to them directly from the cross:

> 'My folk, now answer me
> And say what is my guilt.
> What might I more have done for thee,
> That I have not fulfilled'.

Those lines come from the Common Place book belonging to
a fourteenth century Franciscan friar, John Grimstone.[6] Since

E

this was a storehouse of material for use in the pulpit they must have often been heard as he went around addressing his various congregations.

But John Grimstone is not content to speak in merely general terms. In an unprinted poem contained in the Passion section of his preaching book he links particular human weaknesses and failings with the figure of Christ on the cross. So, when a person raises his arm to strike another in a fit of temper he should reflect on the right hand of Christ pierced with the nail; when the coveteous man attempts to grasp what does not belong to him he should remember Christ's left hand; and when anyone is content to remain in slothfulness and to make no attempt to persevere he should bear in mind the feet of Christ nailed to the cross.[7]

There is, too, that simple but moving appeal which is to be found in a sermon preserved in a manuscript in the library of Lincoln Cathedral, and which although it really belongs to the eve of the Reformation is, when put into modern English, no less applicable to our own time:

'What fault do you find in me, says Christ, and why do you go away from me and will not keep my precepts and commandments? If I have trespassed against you tell me. See now the goodness of almighty God, and behold the pride of men. We are obstinate and rebel against him: for the hard stones broke in the time of Christ's passion; but our hearts are harder in sin than the stones, for they will not break with contrition. Ever the good Lord who is merciful calls us and says: See I am lifted up on high upon the cross for you, sinful creature, that you should hear my voice; turn to me again and I will give you remission and mercy.'[8]

(iv)

Congregations are for ever wayward; and because efforts by word and mouth to move them to penitence as often as not fell on deaf ears, other attempts were made to touch their hearts by appealing to the eyes. One simple device was to paint a Latin inscription on the wall or pillar of a church underneath a cross or picture of the crucifixion in which Christ himself urged men to amendment of life in words which in English read:

> 'See, man, was there ever such suffering?
> Spurn sin, the cause of my wounds which you perceive.
> See, you who transgress, how you cause me pain.' [9]

Another method was to draw people's attention to what were regarded as particularly grave sins: as for example the failure to observe Sunday. There is in the church of Breage in Cornwall, a rather strange medieval wall-painting showing the wounded Christ surrounded by the tools of various trades, which include knives, combs, shears and fish-hooks, as well as a cart.[10] At first sight one might suppose that here was an artist setting out to portray Christ as hallowing the labours of working-men, or as suffering in the wrongs and injustices done to his people. Both these ideas have a modern appeal, but it seems that they were not at the back of that artist's mind. His chief concern was to show how Christ was injured when men were engaged on Sunday in the trades represented by the tools in the picture, and neglected their duty of attendance at public worship because of secular matters. He was a forerunner of the Lord's Day Observance Society!

Again at Broughton church in Buckinghamshire there is a mural portraying a number of fashionably dressed young men, each of whom holds a part of the body of a dismembered Christ. Here the artist, crudely no doubt to our way of thinking but characteristically for his day and age, strove to convince men of the evil of blaspheming and swearing by the various parts of Christ's body, and to move them to shame and penitence.[11] That such blasphemy was all too common is plain from the rebuke of Geoffrey Chaucer's parson in the *Canterbury Tales:* 'For Christ's sake do not swear so sinfully in dismembering of Christ by soul, heart, bones and body'.

More effective perhaps than any of these as visual aids to penitence were the passion scenes enacted in the mystery plays. The crude realism of these dramatic episodes, as for instance in the Wakefield Plays where the brutal savagery of the torturers in their treatment of the Son of God leaves nothing to the human imagination, could scarcely have failed to make its impact on some of those who watched. The cry of the Crucified as the cross was heaved up:

> 'I pray you people that pass me by,
> That lead your life so pleasantly,
> Heave up your hearts on high',[12]

must undoubtedly have evoked a response from some who had been content to lead their lives so pleasantly, and have succeeded in bringing them in penitence to the cross.

(v)

Chaucer's parson in the *Canterbury Tales* devoted much of the story which he told to the seven deadly sins: pride, anger, envy, sloth, covetousness, gluttony and lust, and to the 'branches and twigs' belonging to each of them. Times change, but those sins remain as potent as ever they were. It is an important part of the duty of every Anglican priest, called as he is at his ordination to be a messenger, watchman and steward of the Lord, to bring his people to an awareness of this and so to penitence. While he must never fail to show the deep compassion of Christ for the sinner, he must also never cease to point out the seriousness of the sin. And to do so with any effectiveness he must be a man of whom it may be said, as it was said of Chaucer's parson:

> 'Christ's lore, and his apostles twelve,
> He taught, and first he followed it himself'.

The Christian layman also has no less a responsibility in this matter both by his own example of life and by his refusal to compromise with worldly standards. To throw in one's lot with the world is to reject Christ and the cross which one accepted in baptism. It is this thought which seems to lie behind the stern language used by the author of the Letter to the Hebrews of those who 'crucify to them the Son of God afresh and put him to an open shame'.[13] 'The New Testament doctrine of the cross of Christ as a baptism is never far from the writer's mind.' [14]

In these days there is an ever-increasing tendency on the part of many of our contemporaries to excuse sin as being part of our make-up for which we cannot be held to be entirely responsible. Again, the gravity of sin is constantly being watered down by the use of terms which render it more respectable. Thus the word 'scrounging' is preferred to the more accurate 'stealing'; 'permissiveness' and 'tolerance' become readily accepted substitutes for 'lust' and 'sloth'; and the giving to another person a piece of one's mind is a polite way of describing what is in reality an outburst of uncontrolled anger.

And still the appeal of the Crucified calls men to the cross in penitence in those haunting words of what remains even nowadays one of the most popular of all English Passiontide oratorios, John Stainer's *Crucifixion:*

> 'I wept for the sorrows and pains of men,
> I healed them and helped them and loved them, but then
> They shouted against me "Crucify! "
> Is it nothing to you?
> Behold me and see:
> pierced thro' and thro'
> with countless sorrows,
> and all is for you:
> For you I suffer; for you I die
> Is it nothing to you, all ye that pass by?'

NOTES

[1] Anselm, *Meditation VII* (quoted in *New Catholic Encyclopaedia,* McGraw-Hill, 1967, vol. x, p. 1060).

[2] Dom T. Symons (ed.), *The Monastic Agreement of the Monks and Nuns of the English Nation* (Nelson, 1953), p. 44.

[3] R. Tuve, *A Reading of George Herbert* (Faber, 1952), p. 24.

[4] Luke 24:47.

[5] Acts 2:38.

[6] C. Brown (ed.), *Religious Lyrics of the Fourteenth Century*, No. 72.

[7] R. Woolf, *The English Religious Lyric in the Middle Ages*, pp. 228–9.

[8] G. R. Owst, *Preaching in Medieval England* (C.U.P., 1926), p. 347.

[9] J. Weever, *Ancient Funeral Monuments* (London, 1631), p. 118 (the translation is mine).

[10] A. Caiger-Smith, *English Medieval Mural Painting* (C.U.P., 1963), p. 56.

[11] C. Woodforde, *A Medieval Campaign against Blasphemy* (in *Downside Review*, vol. lv, 1937).

[12] M. Rose (ed.), *The Wakefield Mystery Plays* (Evans, 1961), p. 336.

[13] Heb. 6:6.

[14] A. Richardson, *Introduction to the Theology of the New Testament* (S.C.M., 1958), p. 349.

VII

REDEMPTION

(i)

TOWARDS the end of the eighth century an unknown sculptor fashioned the impressive stone slab which is now preserved in the church of Wirksworth in Derbyshire.[1] This wonderful Saxon relic is decorated with various scenes from the New Testament, but its interest for us as our thoughts turn to the cross and redemption lies in the fact that in the representation of the crucifixion carved upon it the figure of Christ on the cross is replaced by that of a lamb. Another example of this motif in English art is found in an elaborately carved cross head of about a century later, now to be seen in Durham Cathedral Chapter Library, where encircled in the centre of the cross-piece a lamb stands with its forefoot on a book of the Gospels.

The symbol of Christ as the Lamb of God occurs at a very early stage in Christian imagery. It is found in the catacombs and in the mosaics in several of the churches in Rome, and there are some splendid examples on the sarcophagi in Ravenna. Nothing which has so far come to light in England can compare with these; but that is hardly surprising in view of the fact that a seventh century Council of the Eastern Church had forbidden the replacement of the human figure of Christ on the cross by that of a lamb. The Fathers of the Church who were gathered together at this Council felt uneasy lest the reality of the sacrifice of the cross should be obscured by popular symbolism, and they therefore ordered that for the future instead of the lamb Christ should be shown on the crucifix in his human form so that men would be led 'to the remembrance of Jesus, living in the flesh, suffering and dying for our salvation, and thus obtaining the redemption of the world'.[2]

In spite of this prohibition examples of the lamb on the cross continued to appear; and after all, this was not really so surprising when one recalls how much the function of the lamb in restoring men to a right relationship with God had meant both in the days of the Old Testament and in the early Christian Church. 'Christ, our paschal lamb, has been sacrificed',[3] wrote Paul to the Corinthians; and the picture of the lamb willingly led to the slaughter as the means of man's redemption was a treasured one when the people of medieval England contemplated the cross.

A thirteenth century Sequence used in the Church's worship begins with the line:

'The mild Lamb is spread on the rood',

and it goes on to speak of him as hanging there for our guilt and for our good.[4] So the writer conjures up in men's minds the image of the lamb spread on the cross as though it were an altar, and as being offered upon it for their redemption.

It is a picture which still has its place, as we recognise when we sing the Easter hymn which refers to him 'who gave for us his life' as being 'our Paschal Lamb today'; and when in the Eucharist we offer up the ancient petition: 'O Lamb of God that takest away the sins of the world, have mercy upon us'.

(ii)

Jesus clearly saw his work on the cross as redemptive when, in countering the inclination towards self-seeking on the part of his disciples, he said to them: 'the Son of Man also came not to be served but to serve, and to give his life as a ransom for many'.[5] The writer of the Fourth Gospel in his opening chapter shows John the Baptist as bearing witness to Christ as the redeemer when he openly refers to him as the Lamb of God who not merely bears the sins of others but takes them away; and this same writer is most careful to arrange the order of the passiontide events in his Gospel so as to ensure that the death of Jesus on the cross shall coincide with the slaying of the passover lambs. Paul in his letters also makes much of the metaphor of redemption, and of how by means of it man is restored to that right relationship with God which we call 'reconciliation'. All this brings out the close association between the cross and human redemption.

In the Letter to the Hebrews, it is said of Christ that:

'he is the mediator of a new covenant, so that those who are called may receive the promised eternal inheritance, since a death has occurred which redeems them from the transgressions under the first covenant. For when a will is involved, the death of the one who made it must be established.' [6] It was the idea suggested by this unknown author, of the redemption as being a legal deed, which probably gave rise to a curious form of literary composition that appeared during the later medieval period, and is known as the Charter of Christ.

Several copies of such Charters have survived.[7] Most of them are divided into the usual sections found in legal documents of the kind, and either at the beginning or end bear the title in Latin: 'The Charter of human redemption'. In this charter Christ makes a grant of heaven's unending bliss to all who are repentant. The rent which he asks in return is the observance of the two great commandments: love of God and love of one's neighbour. The witnesses to the charter are those extraordinary events which, particularly in the Passion narrative of Matthew, are said to have taken place at the time of the crucifixion: namely, the earth that quaked and the stones which broke into pieces, the day turned into night and the sun become darkened, the dead who rose out of their graves, and the veil of the temple which was torn in two from top to bottom. Naturally Christ's mother and John, as well as the other bystanders, are included as additional witnesses. There follows a reference to the charter's seal, and a note to the effect that the charter was 'given at Calvary, the first day of the great mercy', that is of our redemption.

One of these manuscripts [8] is actually in the form of an imitation charter and there are two tags at the bottom to which a seal could have been attached. In other manuscripts [9] there is the seal of a heart within a frame or a circle, and a note to the effect that on the reverse side of the seal there should be a pelican pecking her breast with the blood from it flowing on to her young ones who are with her in the nest. The tradition that when other remedies failed the pelican freely gave of its own blood in order to restore to life its sickly young ones provided yet another appropriate emblem of Christ's redemptive work on the cross. So this symbol, known as 'the pelican in its piety', which is to be seen carved in wood in some of our English churches is a further reminder to us of how our forefathers visualised the sacrifice made by our Lord for the sake of man's redemption.

(iii)

Redemption through the cross of Christ has always had in the past an important place in English religious life and devotion. In Anglo-Saxon days Benedict Biscop, abbot of Wearmouth in Northumbria, brought back from Rome a number of paintings to decorate the church of St. Paul at Jarrow, which he had founded. Among them was a pair showing Moses lifting up the serpent in the wilderness and beside it the Son of Man lifted up on the cross, as Bede says, 'most cunningly ordered'.[10] Their purpose was to illustrate the parallel between the Old and New Testaments; and to emphasise the fact that just as in the past men had been redeemed by raising their eyes to the saving sign of Moses, so now they were redeemed by turning to the cross of Christ.

Four centuries later, Archbishop Anselm began one of the finest of his meditations, that *On Human Redemption*, with the words:

'Christian soul, soul raised from bitter death, soul redeemed and freed from wretched slavery by the blood of God: arouse your mind, remember your raising again, consider your redemption and liberation'.[11]

The deep anxiety over those thousands of souls in constant danger of perishing 'for the life of each one of whom the Son of God was willing to die a most shameful death' was expressed not, as might have been expected, by a nineteenth century missionary in regard to the inhabitants of some dark continent abroad, but by a great English bishop of the thirteenth century, Robert Grosseteste, in one of his sermons concerning the people of his own diocese of Lincoln.[12]

Again, when one finds John Myrc in his fourteenth century *Instructions for Parish Priests*, urging that not only shall a sick man be tested as to the firmness of his faith and the genuineness of his penitence, but also that the question shall be put to him:

> 'Believest thou with full good devotion
> On Jesus Christ's passion?
> And how his passion save thee shall
> And by none other way at all?',

one might imagine that the writer was an enthusiast of the eighteenth century Evangelical revival rather than a devout medieval Catholic.[13]

In the revised Book of Common Prayer we are reminded in an ancient Easter Collect, happily once more restored, that it was 'for our redemption' that God gave his only-begotten Son to the death of the cross. Moreover, the only surviving pre-Reformation antiphon which has been preserved in the Prayer Book, even though it is tucked away in the office for the Visitation of the Sick, is the beautiful one:

'O Saviour of the world who by thy Cross and precious blood hast redeemed us: save us and help us we humbly beseech thee, O Lord'.

The note of praise sounded in the final verse of John Dryden's paraphrase of the *Veni Creator Spiritus* may bring this list to a fitting conclusion:

> 'The Saviour Son be glorified,
> Who for lost man's redemption died'.

(iv)

During at least one period in the history of the English Church there was a serious danger that the message of redemption through Christ's death on the cross might be forgotten and replaced by mere moralising. It seems incredible now that an Archbishop of Canterbury, who was one of the most popular figures in the pulpit of his time and whose sermons formed the model for many a preacher in the eighteenth century, could deliver a sermon on the wisdom of God in the redemption of mankind, in which he spoke of the design of the Gospel as 'reasonable', and of the dispensation of God as 'beneficial to us and our interest'. Yet such was the 'good news' proclaimed by John Tillotson. Is that, we ask, all that the cross means? Where is there any Gospel fire or a burning zeal for the salvation of men's souls? Little wonder that the Anglican Church should then have reached almost its lowest ebb.

It is to the credit of those who stand in the Evangelical tradition that it was their predecessors who saw the Church not only as the redeemed but also as the redeeming community. They brought it back to life by fearlessly proclaiming the eternal Gospel of man's redemption through the sacrifice of Christ, and in so doing they:

> 'preached as never sure to preach again
> And as a dying man to dying men'.

To this end John Wesley covered thousands of miles up and down England on horseback carrying with him the good news of redemption through the cross, and obeying to the letter the rule he laid down for others who were to follow him:

> 'You have nothing to do but to save souls:
> Therefore spend and be spent in this work'.

His colleague, George Whitefield, who had once declared that Tillotson knew no more about true Christianity than Mahomet, was so conscious of the hunger of souls for the

Gospel that he took to the practice of preaching in the open air when as at Kingswood, a colliery district near Bristol, there was no church. Such was the effect of Whitefield's preaching of the message of redemption through the cross upon the tough coal miners that the white gutters made by their tears which streamed down their black cheeks were plain for all to see.

Again, many people will recall in the earlier years of the present century seeing the men and women of the Salvation Army standing on some street corner on a Saturday night in every sort of condition of weather, simply because of their devotion for Christ and his cross, and their determination to carry on his saving work amongst those members of society whom the Church failed to touch.

In each and in all of these cases the witness was not borne without some personal danger and cost to the individuals concerned. Nobody can read the *Journal* of John Wesley without being made aware of how often he suffered brutal attacks by the mob, sometimes barely escaping with his life. No one who follows the evangelistic labours of George Whitefield will fail to note those occasions when he was pelted with eggs, or else stoned till he was covered with blood. Nor can we study the early history of the Salvation Army without being reminded of how many of its members, including the women, were the victims of violent assaults by a hostile crowd: some were beaten with sticks, others were knocked down and kicked until they became unconscious, while slanders and abusive language were commonplace.[14] Yet each and all would have regarded this persecution by those who knew not what they did, as but a small sacrifice to be made for the privilege of being allowed to share in Christ's redemptive work.

(v)

When someone remarked to me recently that not much was heard about the cross from our pulpits in these days, I could not help but contrast that criticism of the Church with a piece of advice given me by an old Evangelical clergyman shortly before my own ordination: 'Never preach to your people without mentioning the cross'. Should someone perhaps argue that that old man was getting things out of proportion, my own reaction would be to come down on the side of that Evangelical's exaggeration rather than to follow the pattern of a distinguished preacher of our own time who, in a recent sermon, so far from making any reference to Christ and the cross, only saw fit to mention the name of God in the final sentence.

How right was the Nonconformist divine and scholar P. T. Forsyth, when he wrote in his book *The Work of Christ:* 'The apostles never separated reconciliation in any age from the cross and blood of Christ. If ever we do this (and many are doing it today) we throw the New Testament overboard. The bane of so much that claims to be more spiritual religion at the present day is that it simply jettisons the New Testament, and with it historic Christianity'. Forsyth then adds a note that when one of his friends in a discussion with a member of the 'new theology' group made the comment: 'For me all Christianity turns on the unspeakable mercy of God to my soul in the cross of Christ', the other blankly replied, 'I do not understand it'.[15] This was actually written during the first decade of the present century, but it would be equally true of the 1970s.

We may not warm to the person who waylays us at an awkward moment, as for example in a crowded tube train on London's Underground, and asks us the question 'Are you saved?' There may be an inclination to snigger at some of the rather precious stories in certain of the old-fashioned Evangelical novels and tracts, and to smile at such titles as *Redemptive Tidings* and *The Traveller's Guide from Death to Life*. Nevertheless, it would be tragic if our impatience and our sense of superiority were to lead us to ignore what has always been, and is still, a fundamental part of the Christian teaching: that is of redemption through the death of Christ on the cross.

There is a need to remind ourselves and our contemporaries that the primary meaning of the word 'redemption' is not, as some of my City friends would think of it, as a term on the Stock Exchange, but as the *Oxford English Dictionary* rightly says: 'Deliverance from sin and its consequences by the atonement of Jesus Christ'. That is a dictionary definition; but to get at the heart of what redemption through the cross has really meant in English life and devotion we cannot do better than turn to the lines of a seventeenth century Anglican country parson:

> 'Having been tenant long to a rich Lord,
> Not thriving, I resolved to be bold,
> And make a suit unto him, to afford
> A new small-rented lease, and cancell th'old.
>
> In heaven at his manor I him sought:
> They told me there, that he was lately gone
> About some land, which he had dearly bought
> Long since on earth, to take possession.
>
> I straight return'd, and knowing his great birth,
> Sought him accordingly in great resorts;
> In cities, theatres, gardens, parks, and courts:
> At length I heard a ragged noise and mirth
>
> Of thieves and murderers: there I him espied,
> Who straight, "Your suit is granted", said,
> and died.' [16]

NOTES

[1] B. Kurth, *The Iconography of the Wirksworth Slab* (*Burlington Magazine*, vol. lxxxvi, 1945, pp. 114–21).

[2] Council in Trullo, 692.

[3] 1 Cor. 5:7.

[4] C. Brown (ed.), *Religious Lyrics of the Thirteenth Century*, No. 45.

[5] Mark 10:45.

[6] Heb. 9:15–16.

[7] M. C. Spalding, *The Middle English Charters of Christ* (1914).

[8] Brit. Mus. Add. Charter 5960.

[9] ibid. Ms. Sloane 3292; Ms. Stowe 620.

[10] Bede, *Lives of the Abbots,* ch. 9 (in *Baedae Opera Historica,* vol. ii, ed. J. E. King, Loeb Classical Library, 1930).

[11] Anselm, *Opera omnia* (ed. F. S. Schmitt, *Meditatio 3,* vol. iii, p. 84).

[12] W. A. Pantin, in *Robert Grosseteste* (ed. D. A. Callus), (O.U.P., 1955), p. 179.

[13] B. L. Manning, *The People's Faith in the time of Wycliffe* (p. 41).

[14] R. Sandall, *The History of the Salvation Army* (Nelson, 1950), vol. ii, pp. 174ff.

[15] P. T. Forsyth, *The Work of Christ* (Fontana Library, 1965), p. 133.

[16] George Herbert, *Redemption* (World's Classics, (O.U.P.).

VIII

VICTORY

(i)

AMONG the most interesting of the surviving early English crosses is a tall slender one, almost fifteen feet in height, to be seen at Gosforth in Cumberland. In both its form and its decoration this cross is unique. Its shaft, rounded in shape in the lower part and ornamented by imitation bark, shows us that the craftsman who made it clearly intended it to be a reproduction in stone of a wooden cross. Even more important is the point that he meant to represent the cross to all who should look on it as a living tree: the tree of life.

The curious figures which are carved on the Gosforth cross at the higher stages where it has become four-sided, indicate that this is a monument dating from the time when there were colonies of Norsemen living in north-west England. Various explanations have been given as to the meaning of these figures which seem to have been drawn from Nordic mythology; and it is obvious that experts on the subject are greatly divided amongst themselves.[1]

Some interpret them in an entirely pagan sense: thus the central figure in the panel on the east side of the cross is seen as representing Balder, son of the god Odin, the bringer of peace, who was treacherously slain by the blind Hod, one of the figures beneath who bears the fatal spear with which he unwittingly performed the deed, while by Hod's side stands the long-haired Nanna, Balder's sorrowing wife.

Others in complete contrast see these figures in an entirely Christian light: the central crucified figure is for them without any doubt Christ, while those beneath are Longinus the centurion bearing the spear with which he pierced the Lord's

81

side, and Mary Magdalene, who is easily recognisable by her her hair and the alabaster box of ointment which she is holding in her hand.

Still others adopt a midway position and point to the close parallels in the pagan and Christian interpretations. To them it seems plain that when the sculptor carved what was clearly the calm and majestic Balder he did so with the intention of portraying Christ, and that the parallels between Hod who in his blindness dealt Balder the fatal blow, and Longinus the centurion who pierced the side of Christ and knew not what he did, and again between Nanna mourning her beloved and Mary Magdalene standing sorrowfully beside her dead Lord would have been obvious to every Norseman who had been instructed in the Christian faith.

For a Christian believer today who is troubled at finding pagan representations of any kind upon a cross, and who nevertheless is a seeker after the truth the last explanation is perhaps the most satisfying one. We may think of the maker of the great cross at Gosforth as a missionary who carried out his task with an evangelistic purpose in mind. Here was a wonderful opportunity to convey to the Norsemen in England, through a monument which would have treasured associations for them, the message that Christianity had replaced the old Nordic gods and had been responsible for their downfall, and that Christ through his death had triumphed over paganism. In fact the panels on the other three sides of the cross which portray Christ as defeating the devil, as overcoming the world and as triumphant in his glorious resurrection underly the theme, just as they complete the picture.

The Gosforth cross was set up during the period immediately after that which is generally known as the Dark Ages. Those of us Christians who tend at times to be discouraged by the apparent strength of the forces of paganism in the England of today may be heartened by that reflection, and by this fine monument which stands as a witness to the victory of the cross over the powers of darkness and evil.

(ii)

No one who studies the Gospel of John carefully can fail to be impressed by the striking contrasts to be found in its account of the Passion of Christ and in those of the Synoptic writers. While in the latter, especially in the narrative of Mark, the pervading atmosphere is one of humiliation and tragedy, for John the keynote is that of glory and victory.

In the Fourth Gospel it is Jesus himself who takes the initiative. The Synoptic account of the betrayal by Judas Iscariot with the sign of a kiss in the garden is replaced by that of Jesus stepping forward of his own free will to meet those who had come to arrest him. During the actual trial before Pontius Pilate there is a distinct possibility (the Greek word used by John allows it) [2] that Jesus was himself placed upon the seat of judgement by the Roman governor. On the road to Calvary he carries his own cross without any assistance from Simon of Cyrene: indeed the Venerable Bede interpreted the Simon episode as related in the Synoptic Gospels as simply an act of obedience on that man's part to the command of Jesus to take up the cross and follow him. Nothing whatever will make Pilate alter the title which he has caused to be written above the Crucified in the three languages understandable to the whole of the then world: 'This is Jesus the King of the Jews'. And the final cry from the cross in the Fourth Gospel is not as it is in the Markan narrative, one of desolation, but instead a great shout of triumph: 'It is finished',[3] in other words, 'It is fulfilled'. God has indeed reigned from the tree.

The cross as denoting victory, and the Christ upon it as a figure of glory and triumph was undoubtedly the predominating idea in the minds of Christians in the period following the end of persecution by the Roman authorities. Christ through his Church had triumphed over the forces of paganism and darkness. For several centuries that thought was to overshadow completely any association of the cross with humiliation and suffering.

F*

Even as late as the twelfth century one of the most celebrated abbots of the Cistercian abbey of Rievaulx in Yorkshire, Aelred could say in a letter which he wrote to his sister from his monastic cell:

'Behold sister, this very gallows tree is a wonderful sign that Christ is a prince and a most worshipful Lord; as the Book says "the government shall be upon his shoulder", and the cross is "the rod of his righteousness and the sceptre of his kingdom".' [4]

Possibly belonging to the century before Aelred's letter is one of the very few surviving English crucifixes which depict Christ on the cross as triumphant. This is the beautiful one to be seen on the outside wall of the transept of Romsey Abbey in Hampshire.[5] Here is no Christ racked by pain and dying in agony, such as is so familiar to us from the later representations. Instead this figure with open eyes and head erect impresses one by its utter serenity. With the hand of God emerging from the clouds above as if to indicate that the divine purpose has been accomplished through the sacrifice of the cross, the Christ of the Romsey rood proclaims his message to us still: 'Be of good cheer, I have overcome the world'.

(iii)

There are some splendid examples of the cross depicted as the emblem of victory and of the crucified Christ as a triumphant hero in the hymns of Venantius Fortunatus. He was an Italian scholar who lived during the sixth century, and who in his young days studied at Ravenna where he must often have gazed on the wonderful mosaics in its churches and other religious buildings. He would have known that mosaic in the Mausoleum of Galla Placidia which shows Christ the Good Shepherd as a youthful figure seated majestically, dressed in a golden tunic and a cloak of royal purple, and holding in his hand a gold cross almost as though it were a sceptre; and that other mosaic in the Archbishop's chapel featuring the Warrior Christ as he bears a cross on his shoulder and tramples the lion and the serpent under his feet. No one who sees those mosaics even after they have endured the wear and tear of more than fourteen centuries can ever forget them. How much more must they have meant when they were freshly made, and when the message which they proclaimed was generally recognised as being so relevant to the needs of mankind as a whole.

At least it appears that Venantius Fortunatus remembered them in future days when he had left Italy for Gaul, and for Poitiers of which he ultimately became bishop. It was there that he met Radegunde, formerly a Frankish princess, but by that time the abbess of a religious house; and it was for her and for some of the members of her community that he wrote verses which he used to send accompanied by small bunches of flowers or by chestnuts in baskets made by himself.

Fortunatus is one of the people whom I should like to have met, not least because it was he who composed two of the finest Passiontide hymns that have ever been written, two hymns which are still sung in English churches today: 'The royal banners forward go', and 'Sing, my tongue, the glorious battle'. Some idea of the magnificence of that second hymn can be gathered from its opening verse:

> 'Sing, my tongue, the glorious battle,
> Sing the ending of the fray;
> Now above the Cross, the trophy,
> Sound the loud triumphant lay:
> Tell how Christ, the world's Redeemer,
> As a Victim won the day'.[6]

As we sing those hymns it is worth pondering over the thought that they must have reached our shores at an early date. No one knows exactly when they were first sung in the Saxon churches of England by our ancestors of long ago, but Aldhelm, who was bishop of Sherborne at the beginning of the eighth century, refers to hymns which may well have included these; and they were certainly familiar to Englishmen a couple of centuries later.

Several of the actual words and phrases which Bishop Fortunatus used concerning the cross found their way into some of our earliest English poems. Like him, the writers of those poems saw the cross of Christ as 'the one and only noble tree', the 'tree of glory', the 'standard' and the 'sign'. Like him, they rejoiced in the thought that as the first Adam was overcome by a tree, so also by a tree the Second Adam overcame: and by his overcoming brought resurrection and eternal life to all mankind.

(iv)

A person who was to some extent influenced by the ideas found in the hymns of Venantius Fortunatus, and by the place given to the cross in the Church's liturgy of Holy Week was the unknown author of a Saxon poem called *The Dream of the Rood*,[7] which has been described as 'the choicest blossom of Old English Christian poetry'.[8]

The writer begins by telling of how he had a dream, and in his dream he saw a wonderful cross covered with gold and enriched with precious stones: truly a tree of glory shining brilliantly. But even as he gazed on it, it changed its appearance; and behind the gold the poet could perceive a cross stained with blood. He then adopts the effective method of allowing the cross to speak for itself, and to tell its own story. After recalling how, long ago, when it was still a tree growing in the forest it was hewn down and carried away to a hill where it was firmly made fast, the cross continues:

> 'Then I beheld the Master of mankind
> Approach with lordly courage as if he
> Would mount upon me, and I dared not bow'.

Here, indeed, we find ourselves back once more in the setting of the Fourth Gospel, with the Jesus of the Passion narrative taking the initiative of his own accord; and in what follows our Old English poet cannot emphasise too strongly the absolute willingness on the part of Christ and his confidence of victory:

> 'Then the young hero laid his garments by
> He that was God almighty, strong and brave;
> And boldly in the sight of all he mounted
> The lofty cross, for he would free mankind'.

To anyone who comes across *The Dream of the Rood* for the first time, its treatment of the crucifixion theme no doubt seems strange. But is the idea of Christ as a warrior stripping himself as though for battle really so strange? Some of the Fathers did not think so. They saw him, in fact, as a kingly victor removing his clothes for the fray, and not merely as a hero, but a *young* hero as well. Christ's youthfulness no less impressed many of the makers of early Christian sculptures and mosaics. Nowadays, when most of the younger generation regard one as old at forty, the age of thirty-three does not immediately suggest youthfulness. Nevertheless, it represents a comparatively brief period of life, and it was at about that age that Jesus suffered death on the cross.

In the lines which follow, the writer of *The Dream of the Rood* seems to be trying hard to keep the balance between the glorious jewelled cross symbolic of triumph, so familiar to him from its use in the Church's worship during the Easter festival, and the plain blood-red cross symbolising suffering, which was used during Lent and Passiontide. For a moment it looks as though it must be the latter, the tree 'pierced with dark nails' and 'wet with blood', which will prevail. But that is not really the case; for the cross bids the poet tell his dream to men and:

> 'Reveal with words that 'tis the glory-tree
> On which almighty God suffered for sin,
> The many sins of man, and Adam's deed
> Done long ago'

—once again reminding us of the first and second Adam.

This superb poem ends with a reflection on the part of the

writer on this transient life on earth and his longing that the cross will bring him to heaven, the home of the people of God; and with a final prayer that the Lord who once suffered on the cross for men's sins, and who 'freed us' and 'gave us life', will be gracious.

Christ reigning from the cross as a king reigns from his throne: do we today find that difficult to realise? If so, it may be that we like our countrymen during the later Middle Ages, have allowed the triumph-crucifix of an earlier period to be ousted by the crucifix which depicts Christ merely as the human sufferer,[9] and have lost sight of the essential message of the cross and its victory.

(v)

One of my favourite mosaics is that in the apse of the church of San Clemente in Rome, which pictures the cross as a living tree growing on the hill of Paradise. From it branches or tendrils spread out in every direction to invigorate and bring new life and energy to all with which they come in contact. They even enclose in one corner of the mosaic a man who is engaged in the ordinary everyday task of feeding his chickens, and so emphasise the great truth that Christ is the Lord of all life, no matter how humble the person or the task may be.

Even if there is nothing left to us in England which quite matches those heights, the evidence already before us in this chapter is enough to show that for many centuries the men and women of our land visualised the cross not primarily as the instrument of suffering and death, but as the symbol of victory and life. Dr. Michael Ramsey in his book *The Resurrection of Christ*, rightly draws attention to this misplaced tendency in Christian thought and devotion in the past to concentrate on the sufferings of Christ on the cross, and to overlook the aspect of victory. He quotes the words of Bishop Westcott: 'It has been indeed disastrous for our whole view of the Gospel that a late age placed upon the cross the figure of the dead Christ, and that we have retained it there'.[10]

It was Bishop Westcott again who, in one of his *Village Sermons* preached in the early years of this century, wrote:

'If our eyes have been holden hitherto, they need be holden now no longer. Christ is waiting as at this time to reveal his passion and his victory. He holds out to us his cross, the symbol not of suffering only, but of triumph. Let us look to that, and we shall find in it all wisdom and all hope. As we strive to work for God, times of doubt and difficulty, of mistrust and discouragement, must come. It may seem, when we have done all, that the realm of darkness is still unenlightened, the power of evil still unchecked. But let us be of good cheer. Christ reigns from the cross.' [11]

'Christus vincit, Christus regnat, Christus imperat': 'Christ conquers, Christ reigns, Christ rules'. Those who have ever joined with other Christians in this great shout will know the thrill that it brings, and the consciousness of being fellow-sharers with him in his victory.

The theme of this book has been 'The Cross in English Life and Devotion'. Our life would be without purpose or meaning were our devotion to end at the cross. If the poet Venantius Fortunatus, to whom we owe much, could set down those Passiontide hymns, 'The royal banners forward go', and 'Sing, my tongue, the glorious battle', he could also write the glorious processional hymn for Easter morning:

'Hail thee, Festival day! blest day that art hallowed for ever;
Day wherein Christ arose, breaking the kingdom of death'.[12]

The cross, then, is not the end of the story. An unknown Englishman, writing towards the close of the fourteenth century, concludes what is described as one of the most devout of all Passion prayers with the words which each of us in the twentieth century may repeat as his or her own prayer:

'Jesu make me then to rise
From death to life, on such a wise
As thou rose up on Easter day,
In joy and bliss to live for aye,

Amen'.[13]

NOTES

[1] K. Berg, *The Gosforth Cross* (*Journal of Warburg and Courtauld Institute*, vol. 21, 1958).

[2] C. K. Barrett, *The Gospel according to St. John* (S.P.C.K., 1967), pp. 452–3.

[3] John 19:30.

[4] *Aelred's Letter to his Sister* (ed. G. Webb and A. Walker), (Mowbrays, 1957), p. 44.

[5] O. E. Saunders, *A History of English Art in the Middle Ages* (O.U.P., 1932), p. 36.

[6] *English Hymnal* No. 95.

[7] M. Alexander (ed.), *The Earliest English Poems* (Penguin, 1966), contains a modern translation of part of *The Dream of the Rood*, pp. 106–9.

[8] *Cambridge History of English Literature* (C.U.P., 1949, vol. i, p. 57).

[9] G. Aulen, *Christus Victor* (S.P.C.K., 1953), p. 114.

[10] A. M. Ramsey, *The Resurrection of Christ* (Fontana, 1961), p. 117.

[11] B. F. Westcott, *Village Sermons* (Macmillan, 1906), p. 135.

[12] *English Hymnal* No. 624.

[13] C. Brown (ed.), *Religious Lyrics of the Fourteenth Century*, No. 91.